Pinck Development prese

The Think and Grow Rich Workbook
for use with
Think and Grow Rich

This workbook is intended for use with the classic book of achievement Think and Grow Rich, by Napoleon Hill.

For the last five years I have been conducting study groups around the original book, and I created this workbook as a "Teacher's Guide" to help conduct those groups. Though the original book contains the information and techniques required to be successful, I use this workbook as a way to cover the essential material and introduce other information that is relevant to achieving the success of one's chief aim in life.

I have constructed this workbook to follow the organization of the book. Each chapter of the workbook follows the book and is divided into three parts. Text from the original book is italicized and placed under the section labelled "Review." Under the sections labelled "Notes" I have written interpretations and other helpful notes to better understand the chapters. The sections labelled "Exercises" are questions, tools and techniques from the book and other sources I have found to be very useful to help you discover things about yourself that will help you achieve your chief aim in life. After teaching this class for several years, and helping hundreds of people discover the principles in the original text, I feel this book lays out the most effective way for you to understand and start to use the principles shared in Think and Grow Rich.

Though there is space after each question to record an answer, I suggest you use a notebook or journal to record your answers. I have discovered that my desires and wishes have changed over time, and that even one trip through the text or workbook can alter what I initially thought my desires were. Think and Grow Rich is a process of development and each time I expose myself to and use the material, I grow as a person. So will you.

ANYBODY can WISH for riches, and most people do, but only a few know that a definite plan, plus a BURNING DESIRE for wealth, are the only dependable means of accumulating wealth.

© Copyright 2015 by Matt Pinckley

All rights reserved. This workbook is based on the complete and original 1937 version of Think and Grow Rich by Napoleon Hill, originally published by The Ralston Society and now in the public domain. It is not sponsored or endorsed by, or otherwise affiliated with, Napoleon Hill or his family and heirs, the Napoleon Hill Foundation, The Ralston Society, or any other person or entity.

12 Aspects of Wealth

Positive mental attitude

Sound health

Harmony in human relations

Freedom from fear

Hope of future achievement

Capacity for applied faith

Willingness to share one's blessings with others

Be engaged in a labour of love

An open mind towards all subjects towards all people

Complete self-discipline

Wisdom to understand people

Financial security

Note: Money comes last in the list.

Chapter 1 - Introduction

Review

One of the main weaknesses of mankind is the average man's familiarity with the word "impossible." He knows all the rules which will NOT work. He knows all the things which CANNOT be done.

Success comes to those who become SUCCESS CONSCIOUS. Failure comes to those who indifferently allow themselves to become FAILURE CONSCIOUS.

Another weakness found in altogether too many people, is the habit of measuring everything, and everyone, by their own impressions and beliefs.

Our brains become magnetized with the dominating thoughts which we hold in our minds, and, by means with which no man is familiar, these "magnets" attract to us the forces, the people, the circumstances of life which harmonize with the nature of our dominating thoughts.

Notes

In the introduction, Hill introduces us to Ed Barnes, a man with a burning desire to work with Edison, R.U. Darby, a man who quit three feet from gold, and then a little girl who stopped a grown man in his tracks a few years later by refusing to take 'no' for an answer.

There are a few important parts to each of these stories that will help us discover the basic elements to success.

Ed Barnes had to travel from Chicago to New Jersey with just the hope of being able to meet Edison, in spite of the fact that he had no funds to do so. He took a risk that he would not get the opportunity. When he did get the opportunity, it was as a janitor, and took 5 years in that position before his opportunity came. He was humble and persistent, knowing that his opportunity would arise.

R. U. Darby and his uncle headed out west to strike gold. When they had found a small vein, they borrowed money from friends and family, and bought mining equipment to mine more gold from the vein, but the vein ran dry. They drilled and drilled, but did not find gold and quit. A 'junkman' had bought the mining equipment and the claim from the men at a small percentage it had cost them to obtain. He then hired a geological expert to examine the claim, who told him that the vein had shifted just three feet, and if he moved the drills he would strike gold, and strike gold he did, as it was an extremely productive mine. All it took was determination not to quit and the advice of an expert to find gold.

The third person we were introduced to was a small black girl, the daughter of a sharecropper, who used her determination and refusal to accept no as an answer, to subdue a quick tempered white man. Though he had instructed her to leave, and had even indicated he was going to beat her, she stood her ground and got what she wanted. She refused to take no for an answer.

The introduction starts to set the tone of the book, that with a definite purpose, persistence, and a burning desire, one can achieve anything.

Exercise

Answer the following questions as honestly as possible. Do not worry if you think the answers are silly or unrealistic, this workbook is about *you*, what *you* want, and what *you* need to develop to get it.

Is there anyone you know who is like Edwin Barnes, who refused to give up on their dream? Who?

Have you known anyone who quit too soon? Who and why do you think so?

Have you ever known anyone who refuses to take 'no' for an answer? Give an example.

Are you "Success Conscious", and if so, what do you do to maintain that state of mind?

What are the dominating thoughts of your mind currently?

Are you obsessed with any desire? If so, describe what you desire below.

Chapter 2 - Desire

Review

Every human being who reaches the age of understanding of the purpose of money, wishes for it. Wishing will not bring riches. But desiring riches with a state of mind that becomes an obsession, then planning definite ways and means to acquire riches, and backing those plans with persistence which does not recognize failure, will bring riches.

If you truly DESIRE money so keenly that your desire is an obsession, you will have no difficulty in convincing yourself that you will acquire it. The object is to want money, and to become so determined to have it that you CONVINCE yourself you will have it.

Only those who become "money conscious" ever accumulate great riches. "Money consciousness" means that the mind has become so thoroughly saturated with the DESIRE for money, that one can see one's self already in possession of it.

The successful application of these six steps does call for sufficient imagination to enable one to see, and to understand, that accumulation of money cannot be left to chance, good fortune, and luck. One must realize that all who have accumulated great fortunes, first did a certain amount of dreaming, hoping, wishing, DESIRING, and PLANNING before they acquired money.

If you do not see great riches in your imagination, you will never see them in your bank balance.

SUCCESS REQUIRES NO APOLOGIES, FAILURE PERMITS NO ALIBIS.

EVERY FAILURE BRINGS WITH IT THE SEED OF AN EQUIVALENT SUCCESS.

The greatest achievement was, at first, and for a time, but a dream.

Remember too, that all who succeed in life get off to a bad start, and pass through many heartbreaking struggles before they "arrive." The turning point in the lives of those who succeed, usually comes at the moment of some crisis, through which they are introduced to their "other selves."

There is a difference between WISHING for a thing and being READY to receive it. No one is ready for a thing, until he believes he can acquire it. The state of mind must be BELIEF, not mere hope or wish. Open-mindedness is essential for belief. Closed minds do not inspire faith, courage, and belief.

Remember, no more effort is required to aim high in life, to demand abundance and prosperity, than is required to accept misery and poverty.

Notes

Desire is essential to success. Strong desire creates the commitment it takes to overcome the challenges and failures that successful people experience along the way to achieving the goals they have set out for themselves.
Do you know what you desire? Do you know what you are willing to stake *EVERYTHING* for to achieve obtaining it? Do you have a dream that obsesses your mind?

Exercise

In this chapter, Mr. Hill spells out a way for us to obtain what we desire and below is a series of questions to help you formulate and create your own formula for what you desire.

Step One. Write down the exact amount of money you desire. Be definite as to the amount.

Step Two. Determine exactly what you intend to give in return for the money you desire.
Be specific and explain why what you are giving is worth that amount of money. Be convincing.

Step Three. Establish a definite date when you intend to possess the money you desire.

Step Four. Create a definite plan for carrying out your desire. Make sure your plan includes step that you can begin NOW, whether you are ready or not, and put this plan in action, NOW.

Step Five. Write out what it would look like, feel like, and be like if you were already in possession of the money you desire. The more descriptive you are, the better. Write out every detail you can imagine. What would your feelings be when you are in possession of the money? What would the surroundings around you look like? Can you see the bank statement? What clothes are you wearing? Where are you living? What are doing? The more specific the better. You are creating a stage for you to imagine yourself on as you are completing the next step. This is step is very important for you to obtain the amount of money that you desire.

Step Six. Using your answers from the steps above, write out a clear, concise statement of the amount of money you intend to acquire, name the time limit for its acquisition, state what you intend to give in return for the money, and describe clearly the plan through which you intend to accumulate it. Describe the plan as if you have already achieved it, using the descriptions from step five.

Step Seven. Read your written statement aloud from step five, twice daily, once just before retiring at night, and once after arising in the morning. As you read it is important that you see, feel and believe yourself already in possession of the money. Use the details that you created in step six to set the stage for your visualization as you read your statement. If you can, record your voice reading your goal statement out loud, and play this back to yourself twice a day as well.

Chapter 3 - Faith

Review

FAITH is the "eternal elixir" which gives life, power, and action to the impulse of thought!

The foregoing sentence is worth reading a second time, and a third, and a fourth. It is worth reading aloud!

FAITH is the starting point of all accumulation of riches!

FAITH is the basis of all "miracles," and all mysteries which cannot be analyzed by the rules of science!

FAITH is the only known antidote for FAILURE!

FAITH is the element, the "chemical" which, when mixed with prayer, gives one direct communication with Infinite Intelligence.

FAITH is the element which transforms the ordinary vibration of thought, created by the finite mind of man, into the spiritual equivalent.

FAITH is the only agency through which the cosmic force of Infinite Intelligence can be harnessed and used by man.

It is a well known fact that one comes, finally, to BELIEVE whatever one repeats to one's self, whether the statement be true or false.

Every man is what he is, because of the DOMINATING THOUGHTS which he permits to occupy his mind.

THOUGHTS WHICH ARE MIXED WITH ANY OF THE FEELINGS OF EMOTIONS, CONSTITUTE A "MAGNETIC" FORCE WHICH ATTRACTS, FROM THE VIBRATIONS OF THE ETHER, OTHER SIMILAR, OR RELATED THOUGHTS.

A thought thus "magnetized" with emotion may be compared to a seed which, when planted in fertile soil, germinates, grows, and multiplies itself over and over again, until that which was originally one small seed, becomes countless millions of seeds of the SAME BRAND!

Any idea, plan, or purpose may be placed in the mind through repetition of thought. This is why you are asked to write out a statement of your major purpose, or Definite Chief Aim, commit it to memory, and repeat it, in audible words, day after day, until these vibrations of sound have reached your subconscious mind.

Excercise

Our definite chief aim, or purpose, is what gives our lives and actions meaning.

Do you have a **definite chief aim** in life? If so, please write it out below.

If you are struggling with discovering your chief aim in life, do the exercises below to help you discover what it is.

Deathbed Test

The first exercise I suggest using to discover your chief aim in life is called the Deathbed Test. Aristotle is the first known person to suggest this exercise and it is accomplished as follows.

Imagine that you are on your deathbed reviewing your life. What are you reflecting on? What decisions did you make that made a difference in your life, both positive and negative? What did you spend your time doing? Who did you choose to spend your time with? When you die, what will the people in your life remember you for? As you lay there on your deathbed, what is it that you accomplished that brings you the greatest satisfaction of achieving? What could you have done differently? What do you regret? What would you do for or tell the people in your life that you failed to do/say up to that point? What do you wish you had spent more time doing?

Set aside at least thirty minutes to contemplate the idea and questions above and see what you can put into perspective for yourself. Use that information to help create your chief aim in life. The other exercises and ideas in the workbook will help you start to create a plan to achieve those things.

What is your Ikigai?

Ikigai is a Japanese concept that means "a reason for being." The term *ikigai* is composed of two Japanese words: *Iki* referring to life, and *kai*, which roughly means "the realization of what one expects and hopes for".

The word *ikigai* is usually used to indicate the source of value in one's life or the things that make one's life worthwhile. Secondly, the word is used to refer to mental and spiritual circumstances under which individuals feel that their lives are valuable. It's not necessarily linked to one's economic status or the present state of society. Even if a person feels that the present is dark, but they have a goal in mind, they may feel *ikigai*. Behaviours that make us feel *ikigai* are not actions which we are forced to take—these are natural and spontaneous actions.

Everyone has an Ikigai. Finding it requires a deep search of one's self. Use the exercise below to as a start to discovering your Ikigai.

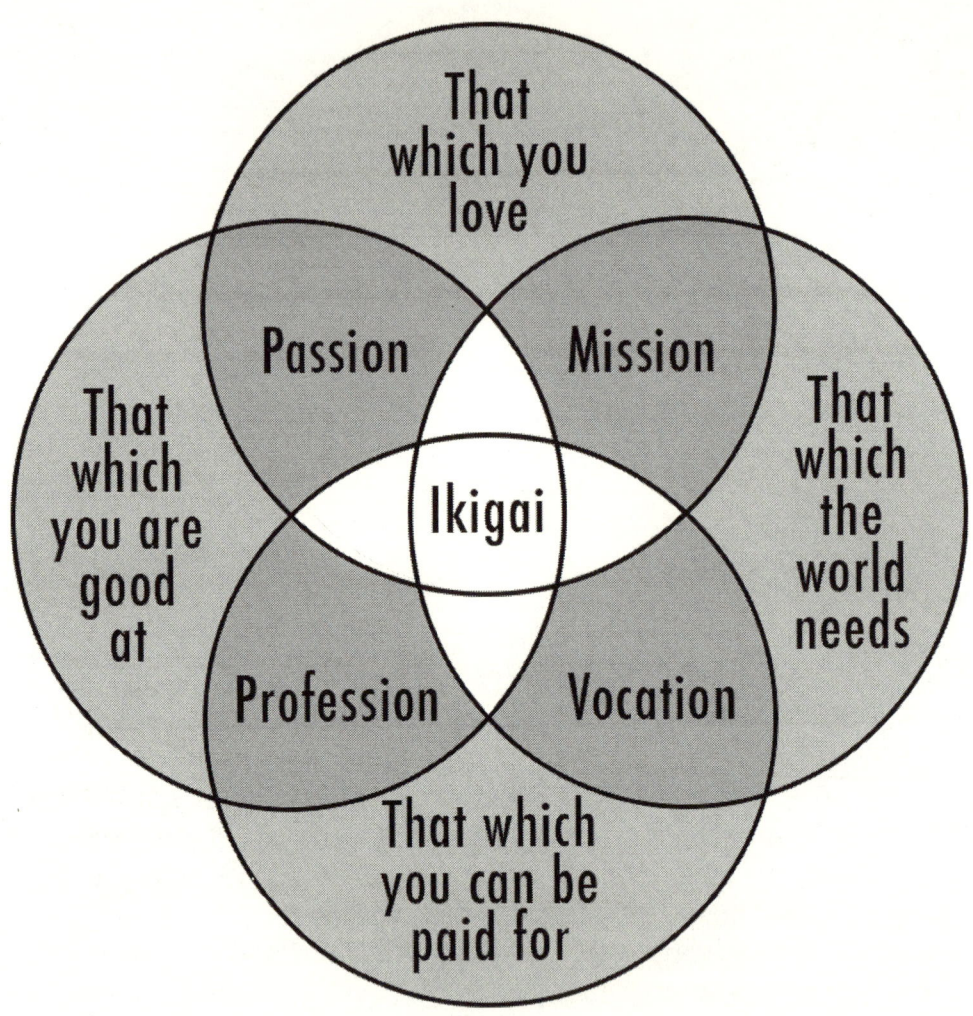

What do you love?

What are you good at?

What can you be paid for?

What is it that the world needs from me?

Some definitions to assist you:

Passion: *an intense desire or enthusiasm for something.*

Profession: *a paid occupation, especially one that involves prolonged training and a formal qualification.*

Vocation: *a strong feeling of suitability for a particular career or occupation.*

Mission: *a strongly felt aim, ambition, or calling.*

Using your answers to the questions above, answer the questions below;

What is your Ikigai passion? (That which you love combined with that which you are good at.)

What is your Ikigai profession? (That which you love combined with that which you can be paid for.)

What is your Ikigai vocation? (That which you can be paid for combined with that which the world needs.)

What is your Ikigai mission? (That which the world needs combined with that which you love.)

The next exercise needs to be completed without interruption, so if for any reason you cannot give yourself 30-90 minutes to do it without interruption, don't attempt it. Turn off the phone, lock yourself into your room, and let everyone know that you are not to be disturbed if there is a chance you will be.

1. Take out a few blank sheets of paper.
2. Write at the top, "What is my true purpose in life?"
3. Write an answer (any answer) that pops into your head. It doesn't have to be a complete sentence. A short phrase is fine.
4. Repeat step 3 until you write the answer that makes you cry. This is your purpose.
5. Write your purpose one more time, making it clear and easy to understand.

This may seem like a simple exercise, but when you approach it with the genuine desire to find your chief aim in life, you will discover what your chief aim or purpose in life is.

Continue writing down things, until the one that makes you tingle and cry comes. It may take several different things to come out before you cry, it may take over 100, 200 or 300 answers. You may want to quit at some point, DON'T, keep pushing through the resistance. Some of the answers may come up more than once, that is okay, as you will take different paths from them each time. Just keep writing answers that come to mind down until the one that makes you cry comes out. You will know it when it happens.

Remember, it does not have to make sense to anyone but yourself. You may not even believe that you can accomplish it or are ready to achieve it, but that is okay. We are discovering what your aim is, not if you can achieve it, though if you desire it enough that it becomes an obsession, you will achieve it, whether or not you are able to right now.

In the space below, using your definite chief aim in life, describe the person you want to become. Be as clear and descriptive as possible. Explain the actions that you take as this person that make you this person.

SELF-CONFIDENCE FORMULA

First. I know that I have the ability to achieve the object of my **Definite Purpose** in life, therefore, I DEMAND of myself persistent, continuous action toward its attainment, and I here and now promise to render such action.

Second. I realize **the dominating thoughts of my mind will eventually reproduce themselves in outward, physical action, and gradually transform themselves into physical reality,** therefore, I will concentrate my thoughts for thirty minutes daily, upon the task of thinking of **the person I intend to become, thereby creating in my mind a clear mental picture of that person.**

Third. I know through the principle of auto-suggestion, **any desire that I persistently hold in my mind will eventually seek expression through some practical means of attaining the object back of it,** therefore, I will devote ten minutes daily to demanding of myself the development of **SELF-CONFIDENCE.**

Fourth. I have clearly written down a description of my **DEFINITE CHIEF AIM** in life, and I will never stop

trying, until I shall have developed sufficient self-confidence for its attainment.

Fifth. *I fully realize that no wealth or position can long endure, unless built upon truth and justice, therefore, I will engage in no transaction which does not benefit all whom it affects. I will succeed by attracting to myself the forces I wish to use, and the cooperation of other people. I will induce others to serve me, because of my willingness to serve others. I will eliminate hatred, envy, jealousy, selfishness, and cynicism, by developing love for all humanity, because I know that a negative attitude toward others can never bring me success. I will cause others to believe in me, because I will believe in them, and in myself.*

I will sign my name to this formula, commit it to memory, and repeat it aloud once a day, with full FAITH that it will gradually influence my THOUGHTS and ACTIONS so that I will become a self-reliant, and successful person.

Chapter 4 - Autosuggestion
Review

AUTO-SUGGESTION is a term which applies to all suggestions and all self-administered stimuli which reach one's mind through the five senses. Stated in another way, autosuggestion is self-suggestion. It is the agency of communication between that part of the mind where conscious thought takes place, and that which serves as the seat of action for the subconscious mind.

Through the dominating thoughts which one permits to remain in the conscious mind, (whether these thoughts be negative or positive, is immaterial), the principle of auto-suggestion voluntarily reaches the subconscious mind and influences it with these thoughts.

NO THOUGHT, whether it be negative or positive, CAN ENTER THE SUBCONSCIOUS MIND WITHOUT THE AID OF THE PRINCIPLE OF AUTO-SUGGESTION, with the exception of thoughts picked up from the ether. Stated differently, all sense impressions which are perceived through the five senses, are stopped by the CONSCIOUS thinking mind, and may be either passed on to the subconscious mind, or rejected, at will. The conscious faculty serves, therefore, as an outer-guard to the approach of the subconscious.

Nature has so built man that he has ABSOLUTE CONTROL over the material which reaches his subconscious mind, through his five senses, although this is not meant to be construed as a statement that man always EXERCISES this control. In the great majority of instances, he does NOT exercise it, which explains why so many people go through life in poverty. Recall what has been said about the subconscious mind resembling a fertile garden spot, in which weeds will grow in abundance, if the seeds of more desirable crops are not sown therein. AUTOSUGGESTION is the agency of control through which an individual may voluntarily feed his subconscious mind on thoughts of a creative nature, or, by neglect, permit thoughts of a destructive nature to find their way into this rich garden of the mind.

Notes

Autosuggestion is at work all the time. Though it is working in our sleep as well, it is easiest for us to identify it during our waking hours. Listen to the stream of thoughts that operate in your mind. Right now you may hear yourself reading these words, you may be thinking of something else, a fantasy, conflict, or other issue that is distracting you from the words on the page, but at all times, our "stream of consciousness" is influencing our lives in a much greater way than we are taught as children. It is that stream of consciousness that influences and programs the subconsciousness with the program or instructions of what to bring about in our lives. As Earl Nightingale says "You become what you think about."

What type of thoughts dominate your mind throughout the day? Do you worry about your situation? Do you think about how you have been slighted? Do you see the lack in your life? Or do you see the abundance in your life? Do you have feelings of gratitude? Do you spend time thinking about how great things are? Where is your mind during the day?

It can be hard to change our patterns of thought at first. If we are in the habit of being critical of ourselves or others, if we see what's wrong with a situation rather than see what's right, if we are judgemental of the people around us, those are all streams of consciousness that we have created that have become habitual in the way we think. There is where the vigilance and persistence that Hill writes about become extremely important. If you are prone to these negative thoughts, you have to retrain your mind not to think that way.

Using the analogy of a stream or river, the stream of consciousness being the river, we need to redirect the flow of that river from feeding the weeds of negativity in our lives to feeding the seeds of abundance and appreciation. It's when we create the new neural pathways, new habits of thoughts, that autosuggestion starts to activate the change in our lives that we need.

Exercises

Our reactions to situations show us a great deal about our tendency of thought. Answer the questions below as honestly as you can. The point of the exercise is not for anyone but yourself to discover your tendency of thought. If you do not know the answer, make note of the question, and witness the answer the next time the situation arises in your life. Then write your answer down.

When you make a mistake, what is your internal dialogue?

When someone else makes a mistake, what is your internal dialogue?

When someone is critical of you, what is your internal dialogue?

When someone slights you, what is your internal dialogue?

When someone compliments you, what is your internal dialogue?

When it is discovered you are wrong, what is your internal dialogue?

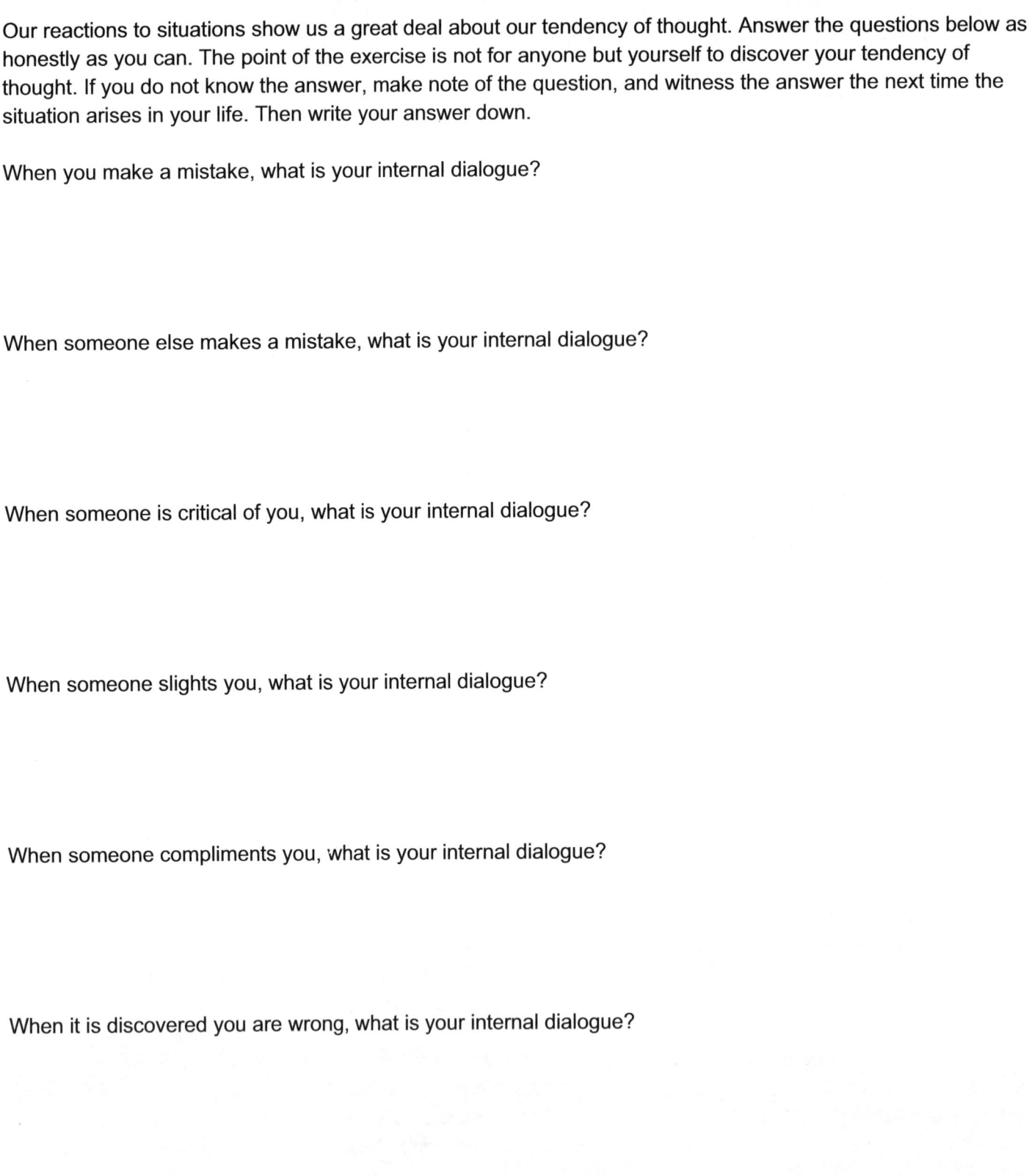

When you walk into a room of strangers, what is your internal dialogue?

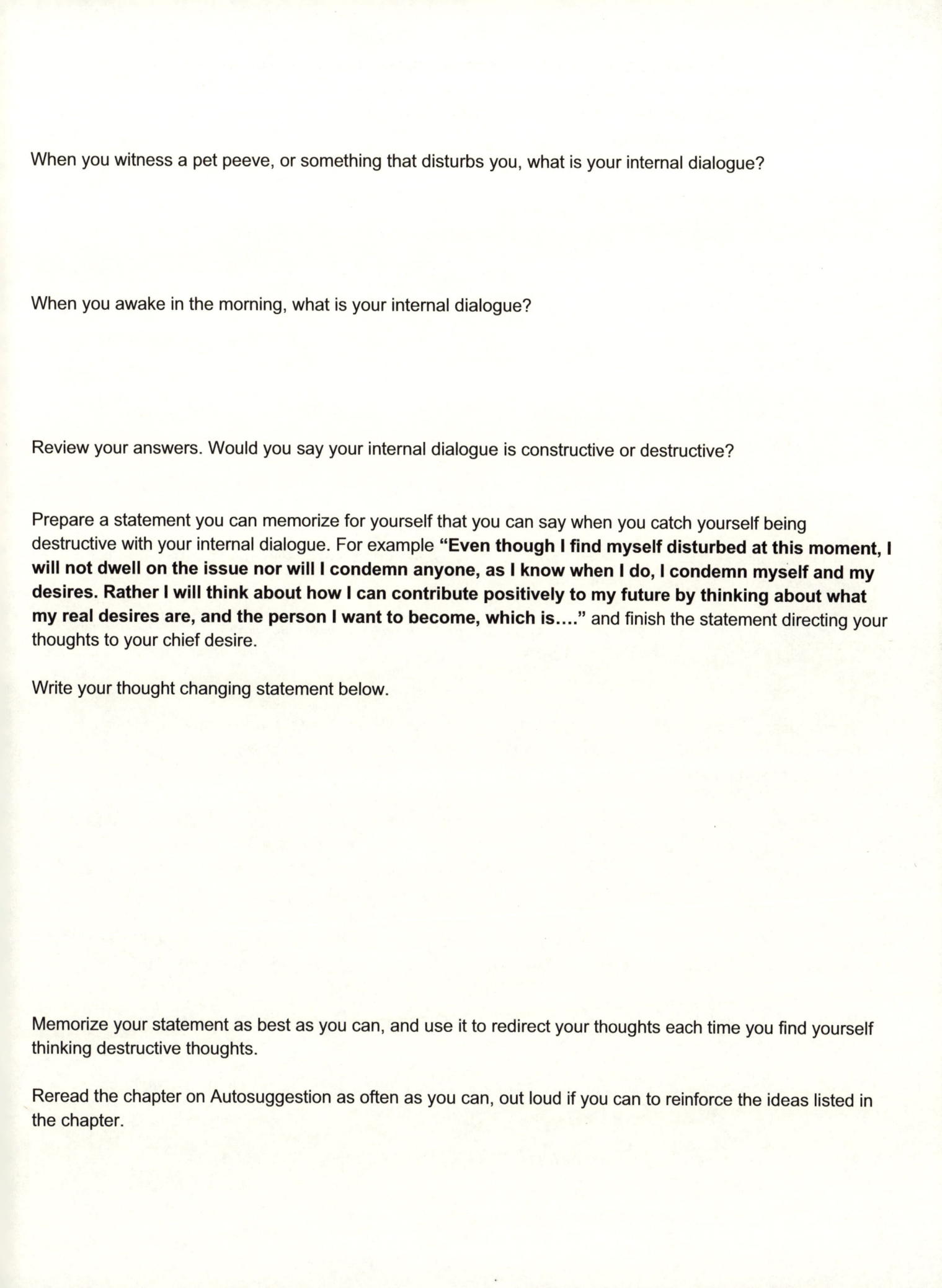

When you witness a pet peeve, or something that disturbs you, what is your internal dialogue?

When you awake in the morning, what is your internal dialogue?

Review your answers. Would you say your internal dialogue is constructive or destructive?

Prepare a statement you can memorize for yourself that you can say when you catch yourself being destructive with your internal dialogue. For example **"Even though I find myself disturbed at this moment, I will not dwell on the issue nor will I condemn anyone, as I know when I do, I condemn myself and my desires. Rather I will think about how I can contribute positively to my future by thinking about what my real desires are, and the person I want to become, which is…."** and finish the statement directing your thoughts to your chief desire.

Write your thought changing statement below.

Memorize your statement as best as you can, and use it to redirect your thoughts each time you find yourself thinking destructive thoughts.

Reread the chapter on Autosuggestion as often as you can, out loud if you can to reinforce the ideas listed in the chapter.

Chapter 5 - Specialized Knowledge

Review

General knowledge, no matter how great in quantity or variety it may be, is of but little use in the accumulation of money.

KNOWLEDGE will not attract money, unless it is organized, and intelligently directed, through practical PLANS OF ACTION, to the DEFINITE END of accumulation of money.

Knowledge is only potential power. It becomes power only when, and if, it is organized into definite plans of action, and directed to a definite end.

Understand the real meaning of the word "educate." That word is derived from the Latin word "educo," meaning to educe, to draw out, to DEVELOP FROM WITHIN.

An educated man is one who has so developed the faculties of his mind that he may acquire anything he wants, or its equivalent, without violating the rights of others.

Any man is educated who knows where to get knowledge when he needs it, and how to organize that knowledge into definite plans of action.

Before you can be sure of your ability to transmute DESIRE into its monetary equivalent, you will require SPECIALIZED KNOWLEDGE of the service, merchandise, or profession which you intend to offer in return for fortune.

The accumulation of great fortunes calls for POWER, and power is acquired through highly organized and intelligently directed specialized knowledge, but that knowledge does not, necessarily, have to be in the possession of the man who accumulates the fortune.

Men sometimes go through life suffering from "inferiority complexes," because they are not men of "education." The man who can organize and direct a "MasterMind" group of men who possess knowledge useful in the accumulation of money, is just as much a man of education as any man in the group. REMEMBER THIS, if you suffer from a feeling of inferiority, because your schooling has been limited.

As knowledge is acquired it must be organized and put into use, for a definite purpose, through practical plans. Knowledge has no value except that which can be gained from its application toward some worthy end.

Successful men, in all callings, never stop acquiring specialized knowledge related to their major purpose, business, or profession.

The truth is that schooling does but little more than to put one in the way of learning how to acquire practical knowledge.

One of the strange things about human beings is that they value only that which has a price.

The person who stops studying merely because he has finished school is forever hopelessly doomed to mediocrity, no matter what may be his calling. The way of success is the way of continuous pursuit of knowledge.

We rise to high positions or remain at the bottom BECAUSE OF CONDITIONS WE CAN CONTROL IF WE DESIRE TO CONTROL THEM.

I BELIEVE THAT CLOSE ASSOCIATION WITH ONE WHO REFUSES TO COMPROMISE WITH CIRCUMSTANCES HE DOES NOT LIKE, IS AN ASSET THAT CAN NEVER BE MEASURED IN TERMS OF MONEY.

There is no fixed price for sound IDEAS!

Back of all IDEAS is specialized knowledge. Unfortunately, for those who do not find riches in abundance, specialized knowledge is more abundant and more easily acquired than IDEAS.

Notes

Does your 'education' help you develop your chief aim, does it help draw out your desire? Or is education something you have acquired, like a cart of books tied to a donkey? The books do nothing for the donkey accept increase his burden, and if knowledge does not contribute to your being then it only increases your burden.

The proper use of knowledge is as important, if not more so, than the knowledge itself.

The idea that learning should be measured by how much "what" you have acquired is ineffective. Rather learning should be measured by how much "how" you have acquired. It is through "how" that change occurs, not "what."

When we use learning to acquire more and more "what" we make great Jeopardy contestants, but when we use learning to acquire more and more "how" we make great artisans, great teachers, great human beings.

Learning 'what' a fishing pole is, is a far cry from learning 'how' a fishing pole works. With the former, you collect knowledge, with the latter, you collect fish.

Exercises

Our society has placed a premium on knowledge, though it is ideas that make people wealthy. We use knowledge to help our ideas come to life, sometimes it is knowledge we possess, sometimes we have to recruit that knowledge. As with Henry Ford, he did not have the knowledge himself, but he had people available to him that do. In the introduction of the book, Darby talked about quitting 3 feet from gold, and though it was a story of persistence, it was also a story of using knowledge correctly.

Does your chief aim in life require any specialized knowledge? If so, what type of knowledge do you require?

What is the plan to obtain that knowledge and how will you organize it?

Do you have ideas that you have not followed up on because you do have not had the knowledge to execute the idea? If so, how could you obtain the knowledge to execute the idea?

Chapter 6 - Imagination

Review

The imagination is literally the workshop wherein are fashioned all plans created by man. The impulse, the DESIRE, is given shape, form, and ACTION through the aid of the imaginative faculty of the mind.

It has been said that man can create anything which he can imagine.

MAN'S ONLY LIMITATION, within reason, LIES IN HIS DEVELOPMENT AND USE OF HIS IMAGINATION.

SYNTHETIC IMAGINATION:—Through this faculty, one may arrange old concepts, ideas, or plans into new combinations. This faculty creates nothing. It merely works with the material of experience, education, and observation with which it is fed. It is the faculty used most by the inventor, with the exception of the who draws upon the creative imagination, when he cannot solve his problem through synthetic imagination.

CREATIVE IMAGINATION:—Through the faculty of creative imagination, the finite mind of man has direct communication with Infinite Intelligence. It is the faculty through which "hunches" and "inspirations" are received. It is by this faculty that all basic, or new ideas are handed over to man.

This faculty functions ONLY when the conscious mind is vibrating at an exceedingly rapid rate, as for example, when the conscious mind is stimulated through the emotion of a strong desire.

The creative faculty becomes more alert, more receptive to vibrations from the sources mentioned, in proportion to its development through USE.

The great leaders of business, industry, finance, and the great artists, musicians, poets, and writers became great, because they developed the faculty of creative imagination.

Both the synthetic and creative faculties of imagination become more alert with use, just as any muscle or organ of the body develops through use.

Desire is only a thought, an impulse. It is nebulous and ephemeral. It is abstract, and of no value, until it has been transformed into its physical counterpart. While the synthetic imagination is the one which will be used most frequently, in the process of transforming the impulse of DESIRE into money, you must keep in mind the fact, that you may face circumstances and situations which demand use of the creative imagination as well.

Center your attention, for the time being, on the development of the synthetic imagination, because this is the faculty which you will use more often in the process of converting desire into money.
Transformation of the intangible impulse, of DESIRE, into the tangible reality, of MONEY, calls for the use of a plan, or plans. These plans must be formed with the aid of the imagination, and mainly, with the synthetic faculty.

The moment you reduce the statement of your desire, and a plan for its realization, to writing, you have actually TAKEN THE FIRST of a series of steps, which will enable you to convert the thought into its physical counterpart.

This earth, every one of the billions of individual cells of your body, and every atom of matter, began as an intangible form of energy.

When you begin with the thought impulse, DESIRE, to accumulate money, you are drafting into your service the same "stuff" that Nature used in creating this earth, and every material form in the universe, including the body and brain in which the thought impulses function.

You are now engaged in the task of trying to profit by Nature's method. You are (sincerely and earnestly, we hope), trying to adapt yourself to Nature's laws, by endeavoring to convert DESIRE into its physical or monetary equivalent.

Do not become discouraged if you do not fully comprehend all that has been stated. Unless you have long been a student of the mind, it is not to be expected that you will assimilate all that is in this chapter upon a first reading.

Whoever you are, wherever you may live, whatever occupation you may be engaged in, just remember in the future, every time you see the words "Coca-Cola," that its vast empire of wealth and influence grew out of a single IDEA, and that the mysterious ingredient the drug clerk—Asa Candler—mixed with the secret formula was. . . IMAGINATION!

Being a philosopher as well as a preacher, Dr. Gunsaulus recognized, as do all who succeed in life, that DEFINITENESS OF PURPOSE is the starting point from which one must begin. He recognized, too, that definiteness of purpose takes on animation, life, and power when backed by a BURNING DESIRE to translate that purpose into its material equivalent.

IDEAS CAN BE TRANSMUTED INTO CASH THROUGH THE POWER OF DEFINITE PURPOSE, PLUS DEFINITE PLANS.

Riches, when they come in huge quantities, are never the result of HARD work! Riches come, if they come at all, in response to definite demands, based upon the application of definite principles, and not by chance or luck. Generally speaking, an idea is an impulse of thought that impels action, by an appeal to the imagination. All master salesmen know that ideas can be sold where merchandise cannot. Ordinary salesmen do not know this-that is why they are "ordinary."

There is no standard price on ideas. The creator of ideas makes his own price, and, if he is smart, gets it.

SUCCESS REQUIRES NO EXPLANATIONS FAILURE PERMITS NO ALIBIS

Notes

Ideas are the result of imagination. The great thing about an idea is that you can come up with an idea, share it with other people (Mastermind groups are covered in chapter 10) at no cost, they can contribute and constructively criticize the idea at no cost, and give it back to you. This is why the statement "It takes money to make money" is false. It takes a sound ideas, put into action, and followed through with, to make money. In other words, a plan combined with action and persistence will produce the desired result.

We all have ideas, ideas are cheap. A burning desire combined with an idea is what gives an idea value. The formula for Coca-Cola was already created. The doctor who had created it had a small desire to pay off his debt, but the clerk had a big idea, combined with a burning desire that turned the simple formula into a globally recognized product. In other words, the original idea was not even his, it was what he combined with the original idea (desire, plan, action & persistence) that made Coca-Cola what it is.

Exercises

Synthetic Imagination is the type of imagination we use when we take existing idea, concepts, and plans and arrange them in new ways. An example of that would be the Internet, as it had existed for 30 years before someone created the idea of using it for commercial and personal use.

Do you have any ideas about how to make something better or more convenient? List them below.

Can those ideas contribute to your chief aim in life? How so?

Who can you share the idea with, that will help you develop it, or help you carry out the plan you create to see it contribute to your chief aim?

Creative Imagination is the type of imagination that comes about as a revelation, hunch, or inspiration. Most geniuses have described a process in which they have created a technique to allow themselves to receive these revelations. In most cases, this involves some time of stilling the mind while conscious, and listening for the quiet voice in our mind that is usually drowned out by the reactions to our environment, reactions to our fantasies, and the internal chatter that goes on inside our mind.

The following exercise is intended to help you find that quiet voice inside your mind, but it will take regular practice, as with most muscles, if you haven't been using it, it atrophies. This type of imagination is very important to discovering our chief aim and the most effective way of achieving it, it is imperative that you work on it daily so it can be of use to you.

1) Choose a time that you will not be disturbed. Most people have found the most effective time is shortly after they wake up, as the conscious mind is still and the mind/body is rested allowing for the least amount of internal distractions.

2) While sitting up, close your eyes and unfocus your mind, just observe the thoughts that cross your mind. Ignore the chatter. If you think of an idea or thought that has the slightest inclination towards your chief aim, allow it to develop.

3) The time you spend doing this is up to you, at first it will be difficult to spend much time with your eyes closed thinking of nothing, but as you continue the practice over the next year, it will be easier to sit with your mind quiet and listen for the quiet voice inside your mind to direct you.

4) After you spend the time you can listening to your quiet voice, open your eyes and write down all the ideas that came forth. Do not judge them for their merit, just write them down. Each week review the previous ideas and see what presents itself. Follow up on any idea that helps you achieve your chief aim.

Chapter 7 - Organized Planning

Review

No individual has sufficient experience, education, native ability, and knowledge to insure the accumulation of a great fortune, without the cooperation of other people.

If the first plan which you adopt does not work successfully, replace it with a new plan, if this new plan fails to work, replace it, in turn with still another, and so on, until you find a plan which DOES WORK.

The most intelligent man living cannot succeed in accumulating money, nor in any other undertaking, without plans which are practical and workable. Just keep this fact in mind, and remember when your plans fail, that temporary defeat is not permanent failure. It may only mean that your plans have not been sound. Build other plans. Start all over again.

Temporary defeat should mean only one thing, the certain knowledge that there is something wrong with your plan. Millions of men go through life in misery and poverty, because they lack a sound plan through which to accumulate a fortune.

Your achievement can be no greater than your PLANS are sound.

No man is ever whipped, until he QUITS—in his own mind.

We see men who have accumulated great fortunes, but we often recognize only their triumph, overlooking the temporary defeats which they had to surmount before arriving.

NO FOLLOWER OF THIS PHILOSOPHY CAN REASONABLY EXPECT TO ACCUMULATE A FORTUNE WITHOUT EXPERIENCING "TEMPORARY DEFEAT."

What else, except ideas and personal services, would one not possessed of property have to give in return for riches?

Broadly speaking, there are two types of people in the world. One type is known as LEADERS, and the other as FOLLOWERS. Decide at the outset whether you intend to become a leader in your chosen calling, or remain a follower. The difference in compensation is vast. The follower cannot reasonably expect the compensation to
which a leader is entitled, although many followers make the mistake of expecting such pay.

Most great leaders began in the capacity of followers. They became great leaders because they were IN-TELLIGENT FOLLOWERS. With few exceptions, the man who cannot follow a leader intelligently, cannot become an efficient leader. The man who can follow a leader most efficiently, is usually the man who develops into leadership most rapidly. An intelligent follower has many advantages, among them the OPPORTUNITY TO
ACQUIRE KNOWLEDGE FROM HIS LEADER.

There are two forms of Leadership. The first, and by far the most effective, is LEADERSHIP BY CONSENT of, and with the sympathy of the followers. The second is LEADERSHIP BY FORCE, without the consent and sympathy of the followers. History is filled with evidences that Leadership by Force cannot endure.

Competent 'brains,' if effectively marketed, represent a much more desirable form of capital than that which is required to conduct a business dealing in commodities, because "brains" are a form of capital which cannot be permanently depreciated through depressions, nor can this form of capital be stolen or spent Moreover, the money which is essential for the conduct of business is as worthless as a sand dune, until it has been mixed with efficient 'brains.'

BE SURE THAT YOU ARE WORTH MORE THAN YOU NOW RECEIVE

It is one thing to WANT money, everyone wants more, but it is something entirely different to be WORTH MORE!

Your value is established entirely by your ability to render useful service or your capacity to induce others to render such service.

CAPITAL consists not alone of money, but more particularly of highly organized, intelligent groups of men who plan ways and means of using money efficiently for the good of the public, and profitably to themselves.

Money, without brains, always is dangerous. Properly used, it is the most important essential of civilization.

I have here analyzed the economic advantages of the capitalistic system for the two-fold purpose of showing:
1) *that all who seek riches must recognize and adapt themselves to the system that controls all approaches to fortunes, large or small, and*
2) *to present the side of the picture opposite to that being shown by politicians and demagogues who deliberately becloud the issues they bring up, by referring to organized capital as if it were something poisonous.*

This is a capitalistic country, it was developed through the use of capital, and we who claim the right to partake of the blessings of freedom and opportunity, we who seek to accumulate riches here, may as well know that neither riches nor opportunity would be available to us if ORGANIZED CAPITAL had not provided these benefits.

FREEDOM of which so many people boast, and so few understand. As great as it is, as far as it reaches, as many privileges as it provides, IT DOES NOT, AND CANNOT BRING RICHES WITHOUT EFFORT.

There is but one dependable method of accumulating, and legally holding riches, and that is by rendering useful service.

Exercises

The following exercises are about self inventory in regards to leadership. As organized planning is such an essential part of leadership, it is crucial that you understand your role as a leader, as if you are to achieve your chief aim, recruiting the assistance of others is a key factor of your success in doing so.

Complete the exercises as honestly as possible, as the more honest you can be with yourself through these exercises, the more effective the principles in the book will become.

The following list is the major attributes of leadership as listed in Think and Grow Rich. Next to each attribute, rate yourself from 1 to 5, 1 meaning "needs major improvement" and 5 meaning "Mastered in thought and action" Refer to the text for the meaning of each attribute.

_____Unwavering Courage

_____Self Control

_____Keen Sense of Justice

_____Definiteness of Decision

_____Definiteness of Plans

_____Habit of Doing More Than Paid For

_____A Pleasing Personality

_____Sympathy and Understanding

_____Mastery of Detail

_____Willingness to Assume Full Responsibility

_____Cooperation

Using your assessment above, start with your weakest attributes and dedicate a week of focus and development to each one. Practice only one attribute a week, and do not practice the same one two weeks in a row. If you scored yourself a five in any of the attributes, ask someone close to you who will be honest if they agree, and if they do, then skip that attribute until you have the others up to a 4, then rotate that attribute in with the others.

Below are the 10 major causes of failure in leadership. Review the list, and place a check next to any that you are guilty of. Refer to the text for the meaning of each cause.

_____ Inability to organize details

_____ Unwillingness to render humble service

_____ Expectation of pay for what you "know" instead of what you do with what you know

_____ Fear of competition from followers

_____ Lack of imagination

_____ Selfishness

_____ Intemperance

_____ Disloyalty

_____ Emphasis of the "Authority" of leadership

_____ Emphasis of title

Any one of these faults is sufficient to induce failure, for that reason it is important that you are honest with yourself about this list. I suggest you reproduce it, take it to the people who look to you for guidance, people you follow, and people that know you well and have them answer as to if you are guilty of any of these major causes of leadership failure.

If you are guilty of any of these causes, create a plan of action to rid yourself of the cause(s) and carry it out IMMEDIATELY.

Here is an example of a plan to rid yourself of Selfishness:

"Anytime I recognize myself thinking about my interests before the interests of other, I will remind myself that though I may receive some perceived benefit in the short term from my selfishness, in the long term I am acting counterproductively to my chief aim in life. It is in a spirit of cooperation and loyalty that I will be able to attract the people who will help me achieve my chief aim, not by acting in my self interest."

Chapter 8 - Decision
Review

LACK OF DECISION is near the head of the list of the 30 major causes of FAILURE

PROCRASTINATION, the opposite of DECISION, is a common enemy which practically every man must conquer.

Analysis of several hundred people who had accumulated fortunes well beyond the million dollar mark, disclosed the fact that every one of them had the habit of REACHING DECISIONS PROMPTLY, and of changing these decisions SLOWLY, if, and when they were changed. People who fail to accumulate money, without exception, have the habit of reaching decisions, IF AT ALL, very slowly, and of changing these decisions quickly and often.

Opinions are the cheapest commodities on earth. Everyone has a flock of opinions ready to be wished upon anyone who will accept them. If you are influenced by "opinions" when you reach DECISIONS, you will not succeed in any undertaking, much less in that of transmuting YOUR OWN DESIRE into money.

Close friends and relatives, while not meaning to do so, often handicap one through "opinions" and sometimes through ridicule, which is meant to be humorous. Thousands of men and women carry inferiority complexes with them all through life, because some well-meaning, but ignorant person destroyed their confidence through "opinions" or ridicule.

You have a brain and mind of your own. USE IT, and reach your own decisions. If you need facts or information from other people, to enable you to reach decisions, as you probably will in many instances; acquire these facts or secure the information you need quietly, without disclosing your purpose.

Notes

I have had to ask a lot of people to make decisions. Watching the different processes people use to make a decision, and seeing the level of success they have in their lives, I have to agree with Napoleon Hill, people who are successful make decisions quickly, and have the commitment and persistence to stick with the decision.

I noticed another thing about good decision makers as well, they are not outcome dependent. They typically believe that no matter the outcome from a decision that they make, as long as a decision is made with sound supporting evidence, they will adjust to whatever the outcome is as a result of the decision they make.

People who make decisions quickly are confident in their purpose and know that even if the decision they make results in setbacks to their purpose, they know they will learn from it and overcome whatever the negative result may be. In other words, their commitment to their purpose carries them beyond concerning themselves with the outcome of making in a decision.

I only ask people who can help me with the decision to help me. People who don't have experience, or are just going to offer their opinion, I avoid, as their opinion will not help me make a decision and often times distracts from the facts and real concerns that need to be considered when making a decision. If they don't have personal experience with the subject at hand, often times their opinions will be based in fear and risk avoidance. It is natural for the people who love us to guide us away from risk, as they do not want to see us hurt or risk the relationship that they have with us, so their opinions are based on their feelings, not fact. Outcomes cannot be controlled, only our behavior, the decisions we make concerning our lives, and our reactions to the outcomes can be. Only by making decisions and learning from those decisions, can we move towards our chief aim in life.

The failure of a making the wrong decision pales in comparison to the failure of making no decision. When the wrong decision is made, one can learn from that decision, and make better ones in the future. The person who makes no decision, does not get the benefit of the education of the decision and fails to understand that even making no decision is a decision, it's the victim's decision, as when you do not make a decision, you are victim to the decisions other people make for you.

Exercises

If you make decisions quickly, you can skip the following exercises..

Write down your chief aim in life.

On a scale for 1 to 10, how committed are you to your achieving your chief aim in life? _____

What is the consequence if you don't achieve your chief aim in life?

When you make the wrong decision, what is your internal dialogue?

When you hear that internal dialogue, who's voice do you hear it in? Is it a parent's? Is it a sibling's of close friend's? Is there a tone to it? Is it ridicule?

Each decision we make is an opportunity to learn, create a script that you can recite to yourself before you make a decision to overcome the fears of making a decision, and a second script, allowing you to be okay with the consequences if you don't make the right decision. Refer to the examples below for help if you need it.

Decision Script: **"I have collected the facts to best of my ability and ignored the opinions of people who can't help me with this decision. Regardless of the outcome, I know that the decision I am making provides me an opportunity to learn the best way of achieving my chief aim in life, regardless of the outcome."**

Outcome Script: *"Though the outcome was not what I hoped for, I can use what I have learned from this decision to help me move towards my chief aim in life. Being wrong does not reflect on me unless I fail to use this learning situation as just that, a learning situation. The decision does not reflect upon what type of person I am, rather what I do with what I learned does."*

Now reflect on what you could have done differently before making the decision to have made a different one. Did you make the decision on bad information, out of misplaced hope, or did you ignore your gut? Use the outcome of every decision as a tool to learn how to make better decisions in the future.

Chapter 9 - Persistence

Review

PERSISTENCE is an essential factor in the procedure of transmuting DESIRE into its monetary equivalent. The basis of persistence is the POWER OF WILL.

What they have is will-power, which they mix with persistence, and place back of their desires to insure the attainment of their objectives.

A few carry on DESPITE all opposition, until they attain their goal. These few are the Fords, Carnegies, Rockefellers, and Edisons.

There may be no heroic connotation to the word "persistence," but the quality is to the character of man what carbon is to steel.

If you are following this book with the intention of applying the knowledge it conveys, your first test as to your PERSISTENCE will come when you begin to follow the six steps described in the second chapter. Unless you are one of the two out of every hundred who already have a DEFINITE GOAL at which you are aiming, and a DEFINITE PLAN for its attainment, you may read the instructions, and then pass on with your daily routine, and never comply with those instructions.

The ease with which lack of persistence may be conquered will depend entirely upon the INTENSITY OF ONE'S DESIRE.

The starting point of all achievement is DESIRE. Keep this constantly in mind. Weak desires bring weak results, just as a small amount of fire makes a small amount of heat. If you find yourself lacking in persistence, this weakness may be remedied by building a stronger fire under your desires.

Fortunes gravitate to men whose minds have been prepared to "attract" them, just as surely as water gravitates to the ocean.

Your subconscious mind works continuously, while you are awake, and while you are asleep.

Spasmodic, or occasional effort to apply the rules will be of no value to you. To get RESULTS, you must apply all of the rules until their application becomes a fixed habit with you.

POVERTY CONSCIOUSNESS WILL VOLUNTARILY SEIZE THE MIND WHICH IS NOT OCCUPIED WITH THE MONEY CONSCIOUSNESS. A poverty consciousness develops without conscious application of habits favorable to it. The money consciousness must be created to order, unless one is born with such a consciousness.

Those who have cultivated the HABIT of persistence seem to enjoy insurance against failure. No matter how many times they are defeated, they finally arrive up toward the top of the ladder.

Those who can "take it" are bountifully rewarded for their PERSISTENCE. They receive, as their compensation, whatever goal they are pursuing. That is not all! They receive something infinitely more important than material compensation—the knowledge that "EVERY FAILURE BRINGS WITH IT THE SEED OF AN EQUIVALENT ADVANTAGE."

We see the few who take the punishment of defeat as an urge to greater effort. These, fortunately, never learn to accept Life's reverse gear. But what we DO NOT SEE, what most of us never suspect of existing, is the silent but irresistible POWER which comes to the rescue of those who fight on in the face of discouragement. If we speak of this power at all we call it PERSISTENCE, and let it go at that. One thing we all know, if one does not possess PERSISTENCE, one does not achieve noteworthy success in any calling.

Persistence is a state of mind, therefore it can be cultivated. Like all states of mind, persistence is based upon definite causes, among them these:—

> a. DEFINITENESS OF PURPOSE. Knowing what one wants is the first and, perhaps, the most important step toward the development of persistence. A strong motive forces one to surmount many difficulties.
>
> b. DESIRE. It is comparatively easy to acquire and to maintain persistence in pursuing the object of intense desire.
>
> c. SELF-RELIANCE. Belief in one's ability to carry out a plan encourages one to follow the plan through with persistence. (Self-reliance can be developed through the principle described in the chapter on autosuggestion).
>
> d. DEFINITENESS OF PLANS. Organized plans, even though they may be weak and entirely impractical, encourage persistence.
>
> e. ACCURATE KNOWLEDGE. Knowing that one's plans are sound, based upon experience or observation, encourages persistence; "guessing" instead of "knowing" destroys persistence.
>
> f. CO-OPERATION. Sympathy, understanding, and harmonious cooperation with others tend to develop persistence.
>
> g. WILL-POWER. The habit of concentrating one's thoughts upon the building of plans for the attainment of a definite purpose, leads to persistence.
>
> h. HABIT. Persistence is the direct result of habit. The mind absorbs and becomes a part of the daily experiences upon which it feeds. Fear, the worst of all enemies, can be effectively cured by forced repetition of acts of courage. Everyone who has seen active service in war knows this.

MOST IDEAS ARE STILLBORN, AND NEED THE BREATH OF LIFE INJECTED INTO THEM THROUGH DEFINITE PLANS OF IMMEDIATE ACTION.

The FEAR OF CRITICISM is at the bottom of the destruction of most ideas which never reach the PLANNING and ACTION stage.

I had the happy privilege of analyzing both Mr. Edison and Mr. Ford, year by year, over a long period of years, and therefore, the opportunity to study them at close range, so I speak from actual knowledge when I say that I found no quality save PERSISTENCE, in either of them, that even remotely suggested the major source of their stupendous achievements.

As one makes an impartial study of the prophets, philosophers, "miracle" men, and religious leaders of the past, one is drawn to the inevitable conclusion that PERSISTENCE, concentration of effort, and DEFINITENESS OF PURPOSE, were the major sources of their achievements.

Notes

Persistence is the hallmark of greatness. We all enjoy the fruits of other's persistence. The light that is lighting the room I type this in is a result of Edison's persistence.

In sales, persistence is the single greatest factor that determines if someone will be successful, and the commitment that someone has to a cause can only be determined by his persistence to achieve the desire that drives that cause.

We all have moments of doubt. When our plans are failing and we reach the point that most men would have quit before they ever reached, we push through. Those who share the glory of success, pushed past their self doubt, made new plans, and tried again. Every great person has had to push themselves and do the things that others would not. If you want to be successful, be prepared to have your commitment tested.

Commitment is the key to persistence. What are you committed to, why are you committed to it, and what are you willing to sacrifice to keep that commitment. Great leaders, great thinkers, and great people commit themselves to their chief aim in life and keep that commitment no matter the challenge or cost.

Exercises

Below is the list that Hill provided of the symptoms of lack of persistence. Go through the list, take inventory of yourself, and place a checkmark next to any of the symptoms you may be guilty. These are weaknesses that must be mastered, and if you find you have any of them, start immediately to rid yourself of them.

_____1. Failure to recognize and to clearly define exactly what one wants.

_____2. Procrastination, with or without cause. (Usually backed up with a formidable array of alibis and excuses).

_____3. Lack of interest in acquiring specialized knowledge.

_____4. Indecision, the habit of "passing the buck" on all occasions, instead of facing issues squarely. (Also backed by alibis).

_____5. The habit of relying upon alibis instead of creating definite plans for the solution of problems.

_____6. Self-satisfaction. There is but little remedy for this affliction, and no hope for those who suffer from it.

_____7. Indifference, usually reflected in one's readiness to compromise on all occasions, rather than meet opposition and fight it.

_____8. The habit of blaming others for one's mistakes, and accepting unfavorable circumstances as being unavoidable.

_____9. WEAKNESS OF DESIRE, due to neglect in the choice of MOTIVES that impel action.

_____10. Willingness, even eagerness, to quit at the first sign of defeat. (Based upon one or more of the 6 basic fears).

_____11. Lack of ORGANIZED PLANS, placed in writing where they may be analyzed.

_____12. The habit of neglecting to move on ideas, or to grasp opportunity when it presents itself.

_____13. WISHING instead of WILLING.

_____14. The habit of compromising with POVERTY instead of aiming at riches. General absence of ambition to be, to do, and to own.

_____15. Searching for all the shortcuts to riches, trying to GET without GIVING a fair equivalent, usually reflected in the habit of gambling, endeavoring to drive "sharp" bargains.

_____16. FEAR OF CRITICISM, failure to create plans and to put them into action, because of what other people will think, do, or say. This enemy belongs at the head of the list, because it generally exists in one's subconscious mind, where its presence is not recognized. (See the Six Basic Fears)

The following steps are what Hill prescribes as the way to create the habit of persistence.

   1. A DEFINITE PURPOSE BACKED BY BURNING DESIRE FOR ITS FULFILLMENT.

   2. A DEFINITE PLAN, EXPRESSED IN CONTINUOUS ACTION.

   3. A MIND CLOSED TIGHTLY AGAINST ALL NEGATIVE AND DISCOURAGING INFLUENCES, including negative suggestions of relatives, friends and acquaintances.

   4. A FRIENDLY ALLIANCE WITH ONE OR MORE PERSONS WHO WILL ENCOURAGE ONE TO FOLLOW THROUGH WITH BOTH PLAN AND PURPOSE.

If you have taken the exercises to heart, the first three should already be part of your daily life. In the next chapter we discuss the importance of the correct Mastermind alliance for ourselves.
If you have not fulfilled the first three steps, stop here and accomplish them, as you will not provide the Mastermind alliance that you participate with the needed contribution. What's worse, you may even create or be part of the wrong Mastermind alliance, as you will not have a concrete foundation to build one on.

Hill goes on to say about the steps above:

These four steps are essential for success in all walks of life. The entire purpose of the thirteen principles of this philosophy is to enable one to take these four steps as a matter of habit.

These are the steps by which one may control one's economic destiny.

They are the steps that lead to freedom and independence of thought.

They are the steps that lead to riches, in small or great quantities.

They lead the way to power, fame, and worldly recognition.

They are the four steps which guarantee favorable "breaks."

They are the steps that convert dreams into physical realities.

They lead, also, to the mastery of FEAR, DISCOURAGEMENT, INDIFFERENCE.

Chapter 10 - Power of the Mastermind
Review

POWER is essential for success in the accumulation of money.

POWER may be defined as "organized and intelligently directed KNOWLEDGE." Power, as the term is here used, refers to ORGANIZED effort, sufficient to enable an individual to transmute DESIRE into its monetary equivalent. ORGANIZED effort is produced through the coordination of effort of two or more people, who work toward a DEFINITE end, in a spirit of harmony.

POWER IS REQUIRED FOR THE ACCUMULATION OF MONEY! POWER IS NECESSARY FOR THE RETENTION OF MONEY AFTER IT HAS BEEN ACCUMULATED!

Let us ascertain how power may be acquired. If power is "organized knowledge," let us examine the sources of knowledge:

a. INFINITE INTELLIGENCE. This source of knowledge may be contacted through the procedure described in another chapter, with the aid of Creative Imagination.

b. ACCUMULATED EXPERIENCE. The accumulated experience of man, (or that portion of it which has been
organized and recorded), may be found in any well-equipped public library (or Internet). An important part of this accumulated experience is taught in public schools and colleges, where it has been classified and organized.

c. EXPERIMENT AND RESEARCH. In the field of science, and in practically every other walk of life, men are gathering, classifying, and organizing new facts daily. This is the source to which one must turn when knowledge is not available through "accumulated experience." Here, too, the Creative Imagination must often be used.

The "Master Mind" may be defined as: "Coordination of knowledge and effort, in a spirit of harmony, between two or more people, for the attainment of a definite purpose."

In a preceding chapter, instructions were given for the creation of PLANS for the purpose of translating DESIRE
into its monetary equivalent. If you carry out these instructions with PERSISTENCE and intelligence, and use discrimination in the selection of your "Master Mind" group, your objective will have been halfway reached, even before you begin to recognize it.

Economic advantages may be created by any person who surrounds himself with the advice, counsel, and personal cooperation of a group of men who are willing to lend him wholehearted aid, in a spirit of PERFECT HARMONY. This form of cooperative alliance has been the basis of nearly every great fortune. Your understanding of this great truth may definitely determine your financial status.

No two minds ever come together without, thereby, creating a third, invisible, intangible force which may be likened to a third mind.

The human mind is a form of energy, a part of it being spiritual in nature. When the minds of two people are coordinated in a SPIRIT OF HARMONY, the spiritual units of energy of each mind form an affinity, which constitutes the "psychic" phase of the Master Mind.

Mr. Carnegie's Master Mind group consisted of a staff of approximately fifty men, with whom he surrounded himself, for the DEFINITE PURPOSE of manufacturing and marketing steel. He attributed his entire fortune to the POWER he accumulated through this "Master Mind."

GREAT POWER CAN BE ACCUMULATED THROUGH NO OTHER PRINCIPLE!

Through a process which only Nature completely understands, she translates energy into matter. Nature's building blocks are available to man, in the energy involved in THINKING! Man's brain may be compared to an electric battery. It absorbs energy from the ether, which permeates every atom of matter, and fills the entire universe. It is a well known fact that a group of electric batteries will provide more energy than a single battery. It is also a well known fact that an individual battery will provide energy in proportion to the number and capacity of the cells it contains.

A group of brains coordinated (or connected) in a spirit of harmony, will provide more thought-energy than a single brain, just as a group of electric batteries will provide more energy than a single battery.

When a group of individual brains are coordinated and function in Harmony, the increased energy created through that alliance, becomes available to every individual brain in the group.

The list of the chief sources from which POWER may be attained is, as you have seen, headed by INFINITE INTELLIGENCE. When two or more people coordinate in a spirit of HARMONY, and work toward a definite objective, they place themselves in position, through that alliance, to absorb power directly from the great universal storehouse of Infinite Intelligence. This is the greatest of all sources of POWER. It is the source to which the genius turns. It is the source to which every great leader turns, (whether he may be conscious of the fact or not).

This is not a course on religion. No fundamental principle described in this book should be interpreted as being intended to interfere either directly, or indirectly, with any man's religious habits. This book has been confined, exclusively, to instructing the reader how to transmute the DEFINITE PURPOSE OF DESIRE FOR MONEY, into its monetary equivalent.

Read, THINK, and meditate as you read. Soon, the entire subject will unfold, and you will see it in perspective. You are now seeing the detail of the individual chapters.

That power, when successfully used in the pursuit of money must be mixed with FAITH. It must be mixed with DESIRE. It must be mixed with PERSISTENCE. It must be applied through a plan, and that plan must be set into ACTION.

It consists of one's THINKING PROCESS. The positive emotions of thought form the side of the stream which carries one to fortune. The negative emotions form the side which carries one down to poverty.

It can serve you ONLY through application and use. Merely reading, and passing judgment on it, either one way or another, will in no way benefit you.

Poverty may, and generally does, voluntarily take the place of riches. When riches take the place of poverty, the change is usually brought about through well conceived and carefully executed PLANS. Poverty needs no plan. It needs no one to aid it, because it is bold and ruthless. Riches are shy and timid. They have to be "attracted."

Exercises

A Mastermind group is an essential part of success, as it will help you focus your energy and transmute that energy into power for your goal. As Hill stated a Mastermind group is *"Coordination of knowledge and effort, in a spirit of harmony, between two or more people, for the attainment of a definite purpose."*

To create a Mastermind group, it is important that you have recognized and written down your definite purpose.

What is your definite purpose?

Do you know of anyone who has the same or similar purpose? List them out and why you think so.

Do you know of anyone who can help you achieve your definite purpose even though their chief aim, maybe they have skills or experience that is needed to achieve your purpose. List them out and why you think so.

Can you or have you recruited them for participation in a Mastermind group?

How often will you or do you meet?

It is possible to have more than one Mastermind group that helps you achieve your definite purpose. One group could be people who have the same definite purpose, and another could be of people whose definite purpose may be different, but the area of knowledge needed for the attainment of that purpose is the reason they meet. Does the attainment of your definite purpose involve creating or participating in more than one group? If so, list the different groups you think you will need to be a part of to achieve your definite purpose.

As the internet has made it possible to meet with people in different locations, geography is no longer a limit. Meetup.com, Google Hangouts, and programs like Skype make it possible to meet while everyone is in different locations. Get started at once creating/finding the groups that will help you succeed in achieving your definite purpose. Methods you can use to recruit people are talking directly to people you would like to have in your group, advertising on Meetup or Craigslist , posting to Facebook, Twitter, Google+ or other social media sharing site. As most of the options above cost very little or nothing to start, do it immediately.

Chapter 11 - The Mystery of Sex Transmutation

Review

The meaning of the word "transmute" is, in simple language, "the changing, or transferring of one element, or form of energy, into another."

The emotion of sex has back of it the possibility of three constructive potentialities, they are:

1. *The perpetuation of mankind.*

2. *The maintenance of health, (as a therapeutic agency, it has no equal).*

3. *The transformation of mediocrity into genius through transmutation.*

Sex transmutation is simple and easily explained. It means the switching of the mind from thoughts of physical expression, to thoughts of some other nature.

The transmutation of sex energy calls for the exercise of will-power, to be sure, but the reward is worth the effort. The desire for sexual expression is inborn and natural. The desire cannot, and should not be submerged or eliminated. But it should be given an outlet through forms of expression which enrich the body, mind, and spirit of man. If not given this form of outlet, through transmutation, it will seek outlets through purely physical channels.

Scientific research has disclosed these significant facts:

1. *The men of greatest achievement are men with highly developed sex natures; men who have learned the art of sex transmutation.*

2. *The men who have accumulated great fortunes and achieved outstanding recognition in literature, art, industry, architecture, and the professions, were motivated by the influence of a woman.*

The emotion of sex is an "irresistible force," against which there can be no such opposition as an "immovable body." When driven by this emotion, men become gifted with a super power for action. Understand this truth, and you will catch the significance of the statement that sex transmutation will lift one to the status of a genius.

A genius is, "a man who has discovered how to increase the vibrations of thought to the point where he can freely communicate with sources of knowledge not available through the ordinary rate of vibration of thought."

The person who thinks will want to ask some questions concerning this definition of genius. The first question will be, "How may one communicate with sources of knowledge which are not available through the ORDINARY rate of vibration of thought?" The next question will be, "Are there known sources of knowledge which are available only to genii, and if so, WHAT ARE THESE SOURCES, and exactly how may they be reached?"

"GENIUS" IS DEVELOPED THROUGH THE SIXTH SENSE

The reality of a "sixth sense" has been fairly well established. This sixth sense is "Creative Imagination." The faculty of creative imagination is one which the majority of people never use during an entire lifetime, and if used at all, it usually happens by mere accident. A relatively small number of people use, WITH DELIBERATION AND PURPOSE AFORETHOUGHT, the faculty of creative imagination. Those who use this faculty voluntarily, and
with understanding of its functions, are GENII.

When ideas or concepts flash into one's mind, through what is popularly called a "hunch," they come from one or more of the following sources:

    1. Infinite Intelligence

    2. One's subconscious mind, wherein is stored every sense impression and thought impulse which ever reached the brain through any of the five senses

    3. From the mind of some other person who has just released the thought, or picture of the idea or concept, through conscious thought, or

    4. From the other person's subconscious storehouse.

The creative imagination functions best when the mind is vibrating (due to some form of mind stimulation) at an exceedingly high rate. That is, when the mind is functioning at a rate of vibration higher than that of ordinary, normal thought.

The creative faculty becomes more alert and receptive to vibrations, originating outside the individual's subconscious mind, the more this faculty is used, and the more the individual relies upon it, and makes demands upon it for thought impulses. This faculty can be cultivated and developed only through use.

For example, the scientific inventor, or "genius, begins an invention by organizing and combining the known ideas, or principles accumulated through experience, through the synthetic faculty (the reasoning faculty). If he finds this accumulated knowledge to be insufficient for the completion of his invention, he then draws upon the sources of knowledge available to him through his creative faculty. The method by which he does this varies with the individual, but this is the sum and substance of his procedure:

    1. HE STIMULATES HIS MIND SO THAT IT VIBRATES ON A HIGHER-THAN-AVERAGE PLANE, using one or more of the ten mind stimulants or some other stimulant of his choice.

    2. HE CONCENTRATES upon the known factors (the finished part) of his invention, and creates in his mind a perfect picture of unknown factors (the unfinished part), of his invention. He holds this picture in mind until it has been taken over by the subconscious mind, then relaxes by clearing his mind of ALL thought, and waits for his answer to "flash" into his mind.

The human mind responds to stimulation!

Among the greatest, and most powerful of these stimuli is the urge of sex. When harnessed and transmuted, this driving force is capable of lifting men into that higher sphere of thought which enables them to master the sources of worry and petty annoyance which beset their pathway on the lower plane.

I discovered, from the analysis of over 25,000 people, that men who succeed in an outstanding way, seldom do so before the age of forty, and more often they do not strike their real pace until they are well beyond the age of fifty. This fact was so astounding that it prompted me to go into the study of its cause most carefully, carrying the investigation over a period of more than twelve years.

This study disclosed the fact that the major reason why the majority of men who succeed do not begin to do so before the age of forty to fifty, is their tendency to DISSIPATE their energies through over indulgence in physical expression of the emotion of sex.

The desire for sexual expression is by far the strongest and most impelling of all the human emotions, and for this very reason this desire, when harnessed and transmuted into action, other than that of physical expression, may raise one to the status of a genius.

Nature has prepared her own potions with which men may safely stimulate their minds so they vibrate on a plane that enables them to tune in to fine and rare thoughts which come from—no man knows where! No satisfactory substitute for Nature's stimulants has ever been found.

The world is ruled, and the destiny of civilization is established, by the human emotions. People are influenced in their actions, not by reason so much as by "feelings." The creative faculty of the mind is set into action entirely by emotions, and not by cold reason. The most powerful of all human emotions is that of sex. There are other mind stimulants, some of which have been listed, but no one of them, nor all of them combined, can equal the driving power of sex.

Highly sexed people always have a plentiful supply of magnetism. Through cultivation and understanding, this vital force may be drawn upon and used to great advantage in the relationships between people.

The salesman who knows how to take his mind off the subject of sex, and direct it in sales effort with as much enthusiasm and determination as he would apply to its original purpose, has acquired the art of sex transmutation

Transmutation of sex energy calls for more willpower than the average person cares to use for this purpose. Those who find it difficult to summon will-power sufficient for transmutation, may gradually acquire this ability. Though this requires will-power, the reward for the practice is more than worth the effort.

The urge of sex has been grossly misunderstood, slandered, and burlesqued by the ignorant and the evil minded, for so long that the very word sex is seldom used in polite society. Men and women who are known to be blessed—yes, BLESSED—with highly sexed natures, are usually looked upon as being people who will bear watching. Instead of being called blessed, they are usually called cursed.

The emotion of sex is a virtue ONLY when used intelligently, and with discrimination. It may be misused, and often is, to such an extent that it debases, instead of enriches, both body and mind. The better use of this power is the burden of this chapter.

Intemperance in sex habits is just as detrimental as intemperance in habits of drinking and eating. In this age in which we live, an age which began with the world war, intemperance in habits of sex is common. This orgy of indulgence may account for the shortage of great leaders. No man can avail himself of the forces of his creative imagination, while dissipating them.

Sex, alone, is a mighty urge to action, but its forces are like a cyclone-they are often uncontrollable. When the emotion of love begins to mix itself with the emotion of sex, the result is calmness of purpose, poise, accuracy of judgment, and balance.

Reformation comes, if at all, through the heart, or the emotional side of man, not through his head, or reasoning side.

The emotions are states of mind. Nature has provided man with a "chemistry of the mind" which operates in a manner similar to the principles of chemistry of matter. It is a well known fact that, through the aid of chemistry of matter, a chemist may create a deadly poison by mixing certain elements, none of which are in themselves harmful in the right proportions. The emotions may, likewise, be combined so as to create a deadly poison. The emotions of sex and jealousy, when mixed, may turn a person into an insane beast.

The presence of any one or more of the destructive emotions in the human mind, through the chemistry of the mind, sets up a poison which may destroy one's sense of justice and fairness. In extreme cases, the presence of any combination of these emotions in the mind may destroy one's reason. The road to genius consists of the development, control, and use of sex, love, and romance. Briefly, the process may be stated as follows:

Encourage the presence of these emotions as the dominating thoughts in one's mind, and discourage the presence of all the destructive emotions. The mind is a creature of habit. It thrives upon the dominating thoughts fed it. Through the faculty of willpower, one may discourage the presence of any emotion, and encourage the presence of any other. Control of the mind, through the power of will, is not difficult. Control comes from persistence, and habit. The secret of control lies in understanding the process of transmutation. When any negative emotion presents itself in one's mind, it can be transmuted into a positive, or constructive emotion, by the simple procedure of changing one's thoughts.

THERE IS NO OTHER ROAD TO GENIUS THAN THROUGH VOLUNTARY SELF EFFORT!

Every person, who has been moved by GENUINE LOVE, knows that it leaves enduring traces upon the human heart.

Go back into your yesterdays, at times, and bathe your mind in the beautiful memories of past love. It will soften the influence of the present worries and annoyances. It will give you a source of escape from the unpleasant realities of life, and maybe who knows, your mind will yield to you, during this temporary retreat into the world of fantasy, ideas, or plans which may change the entire financial or spiritual status of your life.

One who has loved truly, can never lose entirely.

Dismiss, also, the thought that love never comes but once.

There may be, and there usually is, one love experience which leaves a deeper imprint on the heart than all the others, but all love experiences are beneficial, except to the person who becomes resentful and cynical when love makes its departure.

No experience, which touches the human heart with a spiritual force, can possibly be harmful, except through ignorance, or jealousy.

Love is, without question, life's greatest experience.

Love is an emotion with many sides, shades, and colors. The love which one feels for parents, or children is quite different from that which one feels for one's sweetheart.

The love which one feels in true friendship is not the same as that felt for one's sweetheart, parents, or children, but it, too, is a form of love.

When the emotion of romance is added to those of love and sex, the obstructions between the finite mind of man and Infinite Intelligence are removed.

What a different story is this, than those usually associated with the emotion of sex. Here is an interpretation of the emotion which lifts it out of the commonplace, and makes of it potter's clay in the hands of God, from which He fashions all that is beautiful and inspiring. It is an interpretation which would, when properly understood, bring harmony out of the chaos which exists in too many marriages. The disharmonies often expressed in the form of nagging, may usually be traced to lack of knowledge on the subject of sex. Where love, romance and the proper understanding of the emotion and function of sex abide, there is no disharmony between married people.

The hunter who excelled during prehistoric days, before the dawn of civilization, did so, because of his desire to appear great in the eyes of woman. Man's nature has not changed in this respect.

Men who accumulate large fortunes, and attain to great heights of power and fame, do so, mainly, to satisfy their desire to please women.

It is this inherent desire of man to please woman, which gives woman the power to make or break a man.

The woman who understands man's nature and tactfully caters to it, need have no fear of competition from other women. Men may be "giants" with indomitable will-power when dealing with other men, but they are easily managed by the women of their choice.

NO MAN IS HAPPY OR COMPLETE WITHOUT THE MODIFYING INFLUENCE OF THE RIGHT WOMAN.

Notes

Though some of what Napoleon writes may seem antiquated, I think that the essence of what he is describing is not lost through the ages.

We have all been inspired by someone, and have felt what it feels like to be infatuated with an individual. Though sometimes we have created walls to insulate us from the possible pain of love, because just as it can make us feel so inspired, that same intensity applied in the wrong way can feel devastating.

The idea of intimacy is one that is both desired and feared.

Break the word intimacy down like this "in-to-me-see" and we can see it is actually about vulnerability. If we are going to let someone into our inner selves, we must drop the defenses we have learned and become vulnerable. Most people have gone through life fearing being vulnerable and waiting for someone else to be vulnerable first so they can have a sense of safety before becoming vulnerable. Usually as a result of having been vulnerable first once, and the intimacy not being returned, as it can be very painful, and we cannot help but want to avoid pain.

A book titled "The Evolution of Desire" may better help understand the underlying evolutionary reasons why this chapter is accurate.

The book goes into depth about the evolutionary reasons for procreation, and though simplistic, it helps understand the underlying reasons for sex transmutations and why it exists from an evolutionary point of view.

The idea is this: A man will create enough genetic material in a week to populate the earth a few times over, where women create approximately 400 eggs through the fertile period of their lives. When taking that into consideration, from a purely evolutionary drive, men's evolutionary programming is to get as much seed out there as possible, the need to worry about his mate's genetic quality is minimized, as he can continuously create more sperm well into old age, so being concerned with the genetic attributes that will help the odds of his children to survive is minimal. Man's sex drive is evolutionarily programmed to play the numbers game, not the quality one.

Whereas women have a limited amount of eggs and time they can procreate, quality of the genetic material becomes more important, and the need to be selective about a mate is the priority when choosing a mate. Not only from a genetic consideration, meaning choosing mates that are genetically superior, but from a resource consideration as well, does the mate have the resources, or access to them, that will help the odds of the offspring's survival.

For this reason men cannot turn off their sex drive. If two men are sitting in a coffeeshop discussing business, and a fertile woman passes by, it is hard for them not to be interrupted by the thoughts of sex at that point, after all their evolutionary programming is to play the numbers game. Women on the other hand, particularly while they are in the fertile years of their life, have to be able to turn their sex drive off, if they don't, they risk having sex with a man who will not provide the best genetic material for increasing the odds of the success for their offspring to survive.

The book also goes into the idea of empathy and why women are so much more empathetic than men. Women depend on empathy to be able to detect whether or not a man is willing to commit his time and resources to her and her offspring. The odds of her child surviving while she is pregnant and nursing, increase if he does provide those things, decreases if he does not. Will he be there to help raise the child? Will he split his time between her and another woman, thus lessening the odds of the offsprings survival. Empathy helps her determine those things.

Men on the other hand are not wired towards empathy, as if they were emotional during battle or while hunting, they would be killed by other men less empathetic than them. When men are successful hunting or in war, they create more resources for them and their offspring, making them more desirable mates as access to resources helps increase the odds of survival of their offspring.

So the idea is that women can turn off sex, they need to be selective about mates, but they cannot turn off emotions, as it is a tool that helps them and their offspring survive.

Men other hand cannot turn off sex, as they have the best chance of their genetic line being continued by playing the numbers game, where as they can turn off emotions, as they have to be able to be effective at hunting and war to be able to produce more resources making them more attractive mates.

This is often the reason why there is a "gap" in relationships, one sex doesn't understand what drives the other one. The stereotypical statements of "All he wants is sex" and "All she wants is to do is talk" are often times just the evolutionary expression of behavior we are programmed for.

Another book worth noting here is called "The Female Brain." It goes into the physiological differences between the male and female brain, and the significance of those differences.

For example, building on the idea of empathy being more dominant in women than men, the female brain has more empathetic neurons than the male brain, supporting the idea that empathy is an evolutionary tool for women.

As well, it shares how at different times and stages of a woman's life, her brain and corresponding hormones change, and through that change, she experiences life differently. Being more empathic at younger ages than when she is older, again paralleling the need for empathy to determine if a man is willing to commit the resources while she is pregnant and with small children. After menopause there is no need for this, and the brain physiology in women reflect it, as their is a decrease in the sensitivity to oxytocin, the hormone responsible for activating the empathy neurons.

The book is a great read for anyone, but particularly for women, as it will help explain the physiological reasons for a lot of the feelings and emotions that they are experiencing through different stages of their lives.. It is also good for men to read, as it will help them understand their mates emotional needs and wants better.

One more book I would suggest reading is "Games People Play" by Eric Berne. In it, he outlines the basic tenant of Transactional Analysis, and maps the transactions between two or more different people, and the needs being met within those transactions. It specifically covers the crossed transactions of people that create confusion and stress within relationships. It is a useful tool to understanding other people's emotional needs, our own emotional needs, and the way to help ourselves remove the negative needs of our emotional programming.

The ideas behind Transactional Analysis is that as children we needed emotional strokes as much as we needed physical strokes or food, even if those emotional strokes were negative. Those strokes created a belief system that our sense of reasoning is based on, and in our adult lives we go out and produce situations and relationships that allow us to replay those strokes to validate our identity.

The need for these strokes has been shown in a number of documented cases, most notably in the orphans of Romania. The neglect, particularly of emotional strokes, led to horrifying results. Most of the children's brains when viewed with MRI, showed little activity. It is a painful observation, but one that confirmed Berne's main hypothesis of the need for emotional strokes.

I use this form of psychology in a lot of different areas of my life, not only in the sexual and intimate relationships I maintain, but in the relationships I have as a leader, coworker, and friend. Using the tools provided in Games People Play has helped me achieve the intimacy and honesty that all great relationships are based on.

This particular chapter in Think and Grow Rich, as well as the subject matter in general, always creates some level of controversy.

Each of us have beliefs surrounding the subject of sex, love, and partnership. That is why I suggest reading the books referenced above if you are interested in becoming aware of the underpinning factors the effect all of our relationships. Again, if you are to achieve your chief aim in life and have your desire for wealth manifest in your life, you will need to be able to persuade and convince people to help you achieve it. The better you understand the pillars of great relationships, the quicker you will achieve your goals. At the end of the workbook there is a reading list of books I suggest to read.

Below is the poem "Love", from "The Prophet" written by Kahlil Gibran. The wisdom contained it reflects what Napoleon was sharing with the idea and stimulation of the emotion of love.

When love beckons to you, follow him,
Though his ways are hard and steep.
And when his wings enfold you yield to him,
Though the sword hidden among his pinions may wound you.
And when he speaks to you believe in him,
Though his voice may shatter your dreams
as the north wind lays waste the garden.

For even as love crowns you so shall he crucify you. Even as he is for your growth so is he for your pruning.
Even as he ascends to your height and caresses your tenderest branches that quiver in the sun,
So shall he descend to your roots and shake them in their clinging to the earth.

Like sheaves of corn he gathers you unto himself.
He threshes you to make you naked.
He sifts you to free you from your husks.
He grinds you to whiteness.
He kneads you until you are pliant;
And then he assigns you to his sacred fire, that you may become sacred bread for God's sacred feast.

All these things shall love do unto you that you may know the secrets of your heart, and in that knowledge become a fragment of Life's heart.

But if in your fear you would seek only love's peace and love's pleasure,
Then it is better for you that you cover your nakedness and pass out of love's threshing-floor,
Into the seasonless world where you shall laugh, but not all of your laughter, and weep, but not all of your tears.
Love gives naught but itself and takes naught but from itself.
Love possesses not nor would it be possessed;
For love is sufficient unto love.

When you love you should not say, "God is in my heart," but rather, "I am in the heart of God."
And think not you can direct the course of love, for love, if it finds you worthy, directs your course.

Love has no other desire but to fulfill itself.
But if you love and must needs have desires, let these be your desires:
To melt and be like a running brook that sings its melody to the night.
To know the pain of too much tenderness.
To be wounded by your own understanding of love;
And to bleed willingly and joyfully.
To wake at dawn with a winged heart and give thanks for another day of loving;
To rest at the noon hour and meditate love's ecstasy;
To return home at eventide with gratitude;
And then to sleep with a prayer for the beloved in your heart and a song of praise upon your lips.

Beautiful, isn't it?

Exercise

Study the list below, and come to recognize these stimuli in your life and others. The more you understand them, the better will you not only be able to motivate yourself, the more you will understand other people and help them achieve what they want.

THE TEN MIND STIMULI

1. The desire for sex expression
2. Love
3. A burning desire for fame, power, or financial gain, MONEY
4. Music
5. Friendship between either those of the same sex, or those of the opposite sex.
6. A Master Mind alliance based upon the harmony of two or more people who ally themselves for spiritual or temporal advancement.
7. Mutual suffering, such as that experienced by people who are persecuted.
8. Auto-suggestion
9. Fear
10. Narcotics and alcohol.

Eight of these stimuli are natural and constructive. Two are destructive. The list is here presented for the purpose of enabling you to make a comparative study of the major sources of mind stimulation. From this study, it will be readily seen that the emotion of sex is, by great odds, the most intense and powerful of all mind stimuli.

Do you currently use any of the stimuli to help you achieve your desires?

Can you implement any of the stimuli that you are not using to help you achieve your desires? How so?

Contemplate this chapter, read it again if you need to, and write down any ideas that have come to mind while going over this chapter. By writing those ideas down, you may find that you have ideas to help you better use, or beliefs that are keeping you from being able to use the most powerful stimuli known to man to assist you in achieving your definite purpose.

Chapter 12 - The Subconscious Mind

Review

THE SUBCONSCIOUS MIND consists of a field of consciousness, in which every impulse of thought that reaches the objective mind through any of the five senses, is classified and recorded, and from which thoughts may be recalled or withdrawn as letters may be taken from a filing cabinet. It receives, and files, sense impressions or thoughts, regardless of their nature. You may VOLUNTARILY plant in your subconscious mind any plan, thought, or purpose which you desire to translate into its physical or monetary equivalent. The subconscious acts first on the dominating desires which have been mixed with emotional feeling, such as faith.

THE SUBCONSCIOUS MIND WORKS DAY AND NIGHT.

You cannot entirely control your subconscious mind, but you can voluntarily hand over to it any plan, desire, or purpose which you wish transformed into concrete form.

There is plenty of evidence to support the belief that the subconscious mind is the connecting link between the finite mind of man and Infinite Intelligence. It is the intermediary through which one may draw upon the forces of Infinite Intelligence at will.

The possibilities of creative effort connected with the subconscious mind are stupendous and imponderable. They inspire one with awe.

After you have accepted, as a reality, the existence of the subconscious mind, and understand its possibilities, as a medium for transmuting your DESIRES into their physical or monetary equivalent, you will comprehend the full significance of the instructions given in the chapter on DESIRE. You will also understand why you have been repeatedly admonished to MAKE YOUR DESIRES CLEAR, AND TO REDUCE THEM TO WRITING. You will also understand the necessity of PERSISTENCE in carrying out instructions.

The thirteen principles are the stimuli with which you acquire the ability to reach, and to influence your subconscious mind. Do not become discouraged, if you cannot do this upon the first attempt. Remember that the subconscious mind may be voluntarily directed only through habit, under the directions given in the chapter on FAITH. You have not yet had time to master faith. Be patient. Be persistent.

Remember, your subconscious mind functions voluntarily, whether you make any effort to influence it or not. This,
naturally, suggests to you that thoughts of fear and poverty, and all negative thoughts serve as stimuli to your subconscious mind, unless, you master these impulses and give it more desirable food upon which it may feed.

The subconscious mind will not remain idle! If you fail to plant DESIRES in your subconscious mind, it will feed upon the thoughts which reach it as the result of your neglect.

For the present, it is sufficient if you remember that you are living daily, in the midst of all manner of thought impulses which are reaching your subconscious mind, without your knowledge. Some of these impulses are negative, some are positive. You are now engaged in trying to help shut oil the flow of negative impulses, and to aid in voluntarily influencing your subconscious mind, through positive impulses of DESIRE.

When you achieve this, you will possess the key which unlocks the door to your subconscious mind. Moreover, you will control that door so completely, that no undesirable thought may influence your subconscious mind.

Everything which man creates, BEGINS in the form of a thought impulse. Man can create nothing which he does not first conceive in THOUGHT. Through the aid of the imagination, thought impulses may be assembled into plans. The imagination, when under control, may be used for the creation of plans or purposes that lead to success in one's chosen occupation.

All thought impulses, intended for transmutation into their physical equivalent, voluntarily planted in the subconscious mind, must pass through the imagination, and be mixed with faith. The "mixing" of faith with a plan, or purpose, intended for submission to the subconscious mind, may be done ONLY through the imagination.

From these statements, you will readily observe that voluntary use of the subconscious mind calls for coordination and application of all the principles.

Thoughts which go out from one's mind, also imbed themselves deeply in one's subconscious mind, where they serve as a magnet, pattern, or blueprint by which the subconscious mind is influenced while translating them into their physical equivalent. Thoughts are truly things, for the reason that every material thing begins in the form of
thought-energy.

The subconscious mind is more susceptible to influence by impulses of thought mixed with "feeling" or emotion, than by those originating solely in the reasoning portion of the mind

It is a well known fact that emotion or feeling, rules the majority of people. If it is true that the subconscious mind responds more quickly to, and is influenced more readily by thought impulses which are well mixed with emotion, it is essential to become familiar with the more important of the emotions. There are seven major positive emotions, and seven major negative emotions. The negatives voluntarily inject themselves into the thought impulses, which insure passage into the subconscious mind. The positives must be injected, through the principle of auto-suggestion, into the thought impulses which an individual wishes to pass on to his subconscious mind.

These emotions, or feeling impulses, may be likened to yeast in a loaf of bread, because they constitute the ACTION element, which transforms thought impulses from the passive to the active state. Thus may one understand why thought impulses, which have been well mixed with emotion, are acted upon more readily than thought impulses originating in "cold reason."

You are preparing yourself to influence and control the "inner audience" of your subconscious mind, in order to hand over to it the DESIRE for money, which you wish transmuted into its monetary equivalent. It is essential, therefore, that you understand the method of approach to this "inner audience." You must speak its language, or it will not heed your call. It understands best the language of emotion or feeling.

Positive and negative emotions cannot occupy the mind at the same time. One or the other must dominate. It is your responsibility to make sure that positive emotions constitute the dominating influence of your mind. Here the law of HABIT will come to your aid. Form the habit of applying and using the positive emotions! Eventually, they will dominate your mind so completely, that the negatives cannot enter it.

Only by following these instructions literally, and continuously, can you gain control over your subconscious mind. The presence of a single negative in your conscious mind is sufficient to destroy all chances of constructive aid from your subconscious mind.

If you pray for a thing, but have fear as you pray, that you may not receive it, or that your prayer will not be acted upon by Infinite Intelligence, your prayer will have been in vain.

Prayer does, sometimes, result in the realization of that for which one prays. If you have ever had the experience of receiving that for which YOU prayed, go back in your memory, and recall your actual STATE OF MIND, while you were praying, and you will know, for sure, that the theory here described is more than a theory.

What reason have men to believe that this same energy does not connect every human brain with Infinite Intelligence?

There are no toll-gates between the finite mind of man and Infinite Intelligence. The communication costs nothing except Patience, Faith, Persistence, Understanding, and a SINCERE DESIRE to communicate. Moreover, the approach can be made only by the individual himself. Paid prayers are worthless. Infinite Intelligence does no business by proxy. You either go direct, or you do not communicate.

FAITH and FEAR make poor bedfellows. Where one is found, the other cannot exist.

Notes

**Mind is the Master power that moulds and makes,
And Man is Mind, and evermore he takes
The tool of Thought, and, shaping what he wills,
Brings forth a thousand joys, a thousand ills:
— He thinks in secret, and it comes to pass:
Environment is but his looking-glass.
-James Allen**

From THE EDINBURGH LECTURES ON MENTAL SCIENCE
by Thomas Troward

It is here that we find the importance of realizing spirit's independence of time and space. **An ideal, as such, cannot be formed in the future. It must either be formed here and now or not be formed at all;** and it is for this reason that every teacher, who has ever spoken with due knowledge of the subject, has impressed upon his followers **the necessity of picturing to themselves the fulfilment of their desires as already accomplished on the spiritual plane,** as the indispensable condition of fulfilment in the visible and concrete.

When this is properly understood, **any anxious thought as to the means to be employed in the accomplishment of our purposes is seen to be quite unnecessary.** If the end is already secured, then it follows that all the steps leading to it are secured also. The means will pass into the smaller circle of our con-. scious activities day by day in due order, and then we have to work upon them, not with fear, doubt, or feverish excitement, but calmly and joyously, because **we know that the end is already secured, and that our reasonable use of such means as present themselves in the desired direction is only one portion of a much larger coordinated movement,** the final result of which admits of no doubt. **Mental Science does not offer a premium to idleness, but it takes all work out of the region of anxiety and toil by assuring the worker of the success of his labour,** if not in the precise form he anticipated, then in some other still better suited to his requirements. But suppose, when we reach a point where some momentous decision has to be made, we happen to decide wrongly? **On the hypothesis that the end is already secured you cannot decide wrongly.** Your right decision is as much one of the necessary steps in the accomplishment of the end as any of the other conditions leading up to it, and therefore, while being careful to avoid rash action, we may make sure that the same Law which is controlling the rest of the circumstances in the right direction will influence our judgment in that direction also. **To get good results we must properly understand our relation to the great impersonal power we are using.** It is intelligent and we are intelligent, and the two intelligences must co-operate. **We must not fly in the face of the Law by expecting it to do for us what it can only do through us;** and **we must therefore use our intelligence with the knowledge that it is acting as the instrument of a greater intelligence; and because we have this knowledge we may, and should, cease from all anxiety as to the final result.** In actual practice we must **first form the ideal conception of our object with the definite intention of impressing it upon the universal mind** -- it is this intention which takes such thought out of the region of mere casual fancies -- and t**hen affirm that our knowledge of the Law is sufficient reason for a calm expectation of a corresponding result, and that therefore all necessary conditions will come to us in due order.** We can then turn to the affairs of our daily life with **the calm assurance that the initial conditions are either there already or will soon come into view.** If we do not at once see them, let us **rest content with the knowledge that the spiritual prototype is already in existence and wait till some circumstance pointing in the desired direction begins to show itself.**

It may be a very small circumstance, but **it is the direction and not the magnitude which is to be taken into consideration.** As soon as we see it **we should regard it as the first sprouting of the seed we have sown in the Absolute, and do calmly, and without excitement, whatever the circumstances may seem to require, and then later on we shall see that this doing will in turn lead to further circumstances in the same direction** until we find ourselves conducted step by step to the accomplishment of our object. In this way t**he understanding of the great principle of the Law of Supply will, by repeated experiences, deliver us more and more completely out of the region of anxious thought and toilsome labour and bring us into a new world where the useful employment of all our powers, whether mental or physical, will only be an unfolding of our individuality upon the lines of its own nature, and therefore a perpetual source of health and happiness**; a sufficient inducement, surely, to the careful study of the laws governing the relation between the individual and the Universal Mind.

Exercises

Take a mental "thought" inventory by recalling your previous day. Picture yourself throughout the day, and recall your dominating thoughts. Notice that most of the thoughts you are recalling, have an emotion associated or partnered with them. After analysis, what percentage were positive thoughts and want percentage were negative thoughts? Write down the results.

Negative thoughts accounted for _____% of my thoughts.

Positive thoughts accounted for _____% of my thoughts.

Watching our thoughts is one of the most difficult things we do, as often times we do not think about what we are thinking, we are too identified with the emotion behind the thought to actually observe the thought. The following exercise needs to be practiced throughout the next few weeks or longer, so you can have an idea as to what the majority of your thoughts are, and how to interject positive thoughts to replace the negative ones.

Thought Stops

Following these instructions is a list of "cues", for you to choose from. Cues are tools you will use to be able to stop and recognize what is crossing your mind at the time that you recognize or exercise the cue, as we are creatures of habit, you will need to switch cues every week or so, so that you can continue to "catch" your thoughts.

After choosing a cue, anytime during the day that you either recognize or exercise the cue, stop and take note of several things going on at that moment. First, recall the thought process you were going through at the time right before the cue, then take note of the emotion behind the thought, and then take notice of the environment (location, people, things, and other stimuli) around you as you were thinking that thought.

So after recognizing a cue, the mental inventory would look something like this: "**Right before the cue, I was thinking about _____ and the feelings I was having during that thought process were _____** (pleasant, happy, grateful, funny, sad, angry, resentful, etc., be descriptive). **As I stopped the thought I was in the _____** (bedroom, kitchen, office, yard, grocery store, car, breakroom, etc) **and _____** (spouse, coworker, parent, child, etc) **was there with me. As well, the other things that could have been stimulating my thoughts are _____** (tv, radio, fan, any stimuli affecting your thought process).

If you can, write it down then, if not, at the end of the day recall the "Thought Stops" you did through the day, and report what percentages of positive vs. negative thoughts you had throughout the day.

The idea of this exercise is to catch ourselves in the midst of habitualized thought so we can start to change the negative habit and create new positive thought habits. As negative thoughts fill our minds by default, we need to practice exercises that allow us to catch those habits and create new habits. This is one of the most effective tools I have ever used in observing and creating new habits of thought for the mind.

When you start to use a cue in the beginning of the week, you may notice that you don't catch the cue or recall using it throughout the day, and that is okay. Every morning remind yourself of the cue you have chosen for the week, and a few days in you will start to catch yourself using it. Around the end of the week, you will start to catch yourself with regularity, and then it is time to change the cue. The idea is not to create new habits out if the cues, rather use the cues to catch old thought habits that could be interfering with achieving our chief aim in life.

Cues

This is a list of cues I have found helpful for the exercise. Feel free to think up your own as well. The idea behind a cue is something that interrupts your normal patterns through the day so you can stop and take an inventory of what is happening in your environment, both outside your mind and especially inside your mind.

Hands To Face - Anytime you catch your hands on your face, stop and take inventory.

Hands To Head - Anytime you catch your hands on your head, stop and take inventory.

Doorways - Anytime you are walking through a doorway, stop and take inventory.

Door Handles - Anytime you reach for a door handle, stop and take inventory.

Faucets - Anytime you reach for a faucet, stop and take inventory.

Switching Hand Dominance Doors - Change the hand you use to normally open a door, as you do, stop and take inventory.

Switching Hand Dominance Faucets - Change the hand you use to normally turn on a faucet, as you do, stop and take inventory.

Crossed Legs - Anytime you catch yourself with your legs crossed, stop and take inventory.

Crossed Arms - Anytime you catch yourself with your arms crossed, stop and take inventory.

As You Sit - Anytime you go to sit down, stop and take inventory.

As You Stand - Anytime you stand up, stop and take inventory.

As You Drink - Anytime you take a drink, stop and take inventory.

Human Touch - Anytime you touch another human, stop and take inventory.

Touched - Anytime you are touched by another human, stop and take inventory.

Animal Touch - Anytime you touch an animal, stop and take inventory.

You can create your own as well, any action or stimuli that you can decide ahead of time that will produce an interrupt to your identification with thoughts/emotions so you can observe what is happening at that moment.

If you happen to catch yourself thinking a negative thought, don't condemn yourself, just use the statement from chapter 4 that you memorized to counteract and replace your emotional thought/feeling.

"Even though I find myself disturbed at this moment, I will not dwell on the issue nor will I condemn anyone, as I know when I do, I condemn myself and my desires. Rather I will think about how I can contribute positively to my future by thinking about what my real desires are, and the person I want to become, which is…." Finish the statement directing your thoughts to your chief desire.

Chapter 13 - The Brain

Review

MORE than twenty years ago, the author, working in conjunction with the late Dr. Alexander Graham Bell, and Dr. Elmer R. Gates, observed that every human brain is both a broadcasting and receiving station for the vibration of thought.

Through the medium of the ether, in a fashion similar to that employed by the radio broadcasting principle, every human brain is capable of picking up vibrations of thought which are being released by other brains.

When stimulated, or "stepped up" to a high rate of vibration, the mind becomes more receptive to the vibration of thought which reaches it through the ether from outside sources. This "stepping up" process takes place through the positive emotions, or the negative emotions. Through the emotions, the vibrations of thought may be increased.

Vibrations of an exceedingly high rate are the only vibrations picked up and carried, by the ether, from one brain to another. Thought is energy travelling at an exceedingly high rate of vibration. Thought, which has been modified or "stepped up" by any of the major emotions, vibrates at a much higher rate than ordinary thought, and it is this type of thought which passes from one brain to another, through the broadcasting machinery of the human brain.

The emotion of sex stands at the head of the list of human emotions, as far as intensity and driving force are concerned. The brain which has been stimulated by the emotion of sex, vibrates at a much more rapid rate than it does when that emotion is quiescent or absent.

The result of sex transmutation, is the increase of the rate of vibration of thoughts to such a pitch that the Creative Imagination becomes highly receptive to ideas, which it picks up from the ether. On the other hand, when the brain is vibrating at a rapid rate, it not only attracts thoughts and ideas released by other brains through the medium of the ether, but it gives to one's own thoughts that "feeling" which is essential before those thoughts will be picked up and acted upon by one's subconscious mind.

The subconscious mind is the "sending station" of the brain, through which vibrations of thought are broadcast. The Creative Imagination is the "receiving set," through which the vibrations of thought are picked up from the ether.

Along with the important factors of the subconscious mind, and the faculty of the Creative Imagination, which constitute the sending and receiving sets of your mental broadcasting machinery, consider now the principle of auto-suggestion, which is the medium by which you may put into operation your "broadcasting" station.

Through the instructions described in the chapter on autosuggestion, you were definitely informed of the method by which DESIRE may be transmuted into its monetary equivalent.

Operation of your mental "broadcasting" station is a comparatively simple procedure. You have but three principles to bear in mind, and to apply, when you wish to use your broadcasting station—the SUBCONSCIOUS MIND, CREATIVE IMAGINATION, and AUTO-SUGGESTION. The stimuli through which you put these three principles into action have been described—the procedure begins with DESIRE.
THE GREATEST FORCES ARE "INTANGIBLE"

All of us are controlled by forces which are unseen and intangible.

The whole of mankind has not the power to cope with, nor to control the intangible force wrapped up in the rolling waves of the oceans. Man has not the capacity to understand the intangible force of gravity, which keeps this little earth suspended in mid-air, and keeps man from falling from it, much less the power to control that force. Man is entirely subservient to the intangible force which comes with a thunder storm, and he is just as helpless in the presence of the intangible force of electricity— nay, he does not even know what electricity is, where it comes from, or what is its purpose!

It is inconceivable that such a network of intricate machinery should be in existence for the sole purpose of carrying on the physical functions incidental to growth and maintenance of the physical body. Is it not likely that the same system, which gives billions of brain cells the media for communication one with another, provides, also the means of communication with other intangible forces?

Notes

A lot has been discovered about the anatomy and physiology of the brain since Think and Grow Rich was originally published and it has been interesting to see how most of it confirms what Napoleon Hill wrote.

For example, neurons located right behind your forehead have been discovered called mirror neurons. A mirror neuron is a neuron that fires both when an animal acts and when the animal observes the same action performed by another. Thus, the neuron "mirrors" the behavior of the other, as though the observer was itself acting.

Mirror neurons are neurons that assist you in experiencing the feelings of and have empathy towards other people. Most psychologists and behaviorists agree that we communicate using mirror neurons, that they are responsible for our feelings of compassion, and transmit and receive data that help us learn and process language, customs, and other cultural instructions.

Ever watch someone receive an immunization shot, and as they are going through the experience, you can feel it? That's your mirror neurons at work.

Do you have a favorite sports team? When your favorite sport team scores or wins and you get that surge of feel-good dopamine, that is your mirror neurons at work.

When Napoleon Hill wrote "*that every human brain is both a broadcasting and receiving station for the vibration of thought*" though they had not discovered mirror neurons yet, he and others had observed the behavior enough to know that the brain played a role in how our thoughts influence one another.

When a thought is emotionalized, it enhances the way the mirror neurons respond as well. That's why when we see someone walking or doing something with no emotional value, we have very little mirror neuron response, but when they are experiencing pain, like getting a shot, or scoring a goal, we get emotionalized as well.

The brain is elastic as well, meaning you can change who you are as a result of your brain and with the right practice and commitment, you can bring about the change in yourself and the thinking patterns that will help you realize your desires and move you closer to your chief aim in life.
Have you ever heard the term "Fixed Mindset vs Growth Mindset"?

It expresses two ideas of the way that people see themselves and how they learn.

People with "Fixed Mindsets" believe talent and intelligence are innate, fixed attributes that one is born with, either you have it or you don't. When you hear someone say that they are not good at something, and imply they never could be, they are guilty of the "Fixed Mindset".

Fixed Mindset people tend to not like to take tests or try new things, as if they fail, it will mean that they are a failure, and since talent is innate, they won't take the chances or push themselves beyond the point of comfort.

People with "Growth Mindsets" believe that talent and intelligence are not static, but rather elastic, and can be improved with practice. They typically like challenges, or at least are not scared of them, as they see a challenge as a way for them to improve their abilities and talents.

Brain science has proven that the brain is elastic though, and with practice, anyone can become great at music, math, science, reading, whatever the challenge may be, one can improve dramatically with practice.

As you go through the inventories in the appendix, remember you are not destined or stuck with a limited amount to talent, you get out of your elf what you expect of and put into yourself.

I am sure as we discover more of the science of the brain, we will learn more ways that people's brains communicate with one another and learn how to use them to helping us achieve more and more.

Exercises

Is there any part of your mind that you place a limit on because of a fixed mindset belief? What can you tell yourself to change that belief?

Knowing what you know about feelings and emotions and how they charge our desires, creative imagination, and subconscious, look over your desire statement, sit with it and allow your creative intelligence to go over it, and rewrite it with more descriptive feeling below.

Chapter 14 - The Sixth Sense

Review

THE "thirteenth" principle is known as the SIXTH SENSE, through which Infinite Intelligence may, and will communicate voluntarily, without any effort from, or demands by, the individual.

This principle is the apex of the philosophy. It can be assimilated, understood, and applied ONLY by first mastering the other twelve principles.

The SIXTH SENSE is that portion of the subconscious mind which has been referred to as the Creative Imagination. It has also been referred to as the "receiving set" through which ideas, plans, and thoughts flash into the mind. The "flashes" are sometimes called "hunches" or "inspirations."

Understanding of the sixth sense comes only by meditation through mind development from within.

It is believed to be the point at which the mind of man contacts the Universal Mind.

Through the aid of the sixth sense, you will be warned of impending dangers in time to avoid them, and notified of opportunities in time to embrace them.

The author is not a believer in, nor an advocate of "miracles," for the reason that he has enough knowledge of Nature to understand that Nature never deviates from her established laws. Some of her laws are so incomprehensible that they produce what appear to be "miracles." The sixth sense comes as near to being a miracle as anything I have ever experienced, and it appears so, only because I do not understand the method by which this principle is operated.

This much the author does know—that there is a power, or a First Cause, or an Intelligence, which permeates every atom of matter, and embraces every unit of energy perceptible to man—that this Infinite Intelligence converts acorns into oak trees, causes water to flow downhill in response to the law of gravity, follows night with day, and winter with summer, each maintaining its proper place and relationship to the other. This Intelligence may, through the principles of this philosophy, be induced to aid in transmuting DESIRES into concrete, or material form. The author has this knowledge, because he has experimented with it— and has EXPERIENCED IT.

Step by step, through the preceding chapters, you have been led to this, the last principle. If you have mastered each of the preceding principles, you are now prepared to accept, without being skeptical, the stupendous claims made here. If you have not mastered the other principles, you must do so before you may determine, definitely, whether or not the claims made in this chapter are fact or fiction.

My experience has taught me that the next best thing to being truly great, is to emulate the great, by feeling and action, as nearly as possible.

Such knowledge, generally, is received when the mind is under the influence of extraordinary stimulation. Any emergency which arouses the emotions, and causes the heart to beat more rapidly than normal may, and generally does, bring the sixth sense into action.

My original purpose in conducting Council meetings with imaginary beings, was solely that of impressing my own subconscious mind, through the principle of auto-suggestion, with certain characteristics which I desired to *acquire. In more recent years, my experimentation has taken on an entirely different trend. I now go to my imaginary counselors with every difficult problem which confronts me and my clients. The results are often astonishing, although I do not depend entirely on this form of Counsel.*

The sixth sense is not something that one can take off and put on at will. Ability to use this great power comes slowly, through application of the other principles outlined in this book. Seldom does any individual come into workable knowledge of the sixth sense before the age of forty. More often the knowledge is not available until one is well past fifty, and this, for the reason that the spiritual forces, with which the sixth sense is so closely related, do not mature and become usable except through years of meditation, self-examination, and serious thought.

No matter who you are, or what may have been your purpose in reading this book, you can profit by it without understanding the principle described in this chapter. This is especially true if your major purpose is that of accumulation of money or other material things.

The chapter on the sixth sense was included, because the book is designed for the purpose of presenting a complete philosophy by which individuals may unerringly guide themselves in attaining whatever they ask of life. The starting point of all achievement is DESIRE. The finishing point is that brand of KNOWLEDGE which leads to understanding—understanding of self, understanding of others, understanding of the laws of Nature, recognition and understanding of HAPPINESS.

This sort of understanding comes in its fullness only through familiarity with, and use of the principle of the sixth sense, hence that principle had to be included as a part of this philosophy, for the benefit of those who demand more than money.

Then you will be in position to transmute your DESIRES into their physical or financial counterpart as easily as you may lie down and quit at the first sign of opposition.

Search yourself carefully as you study these six enemies, as they may exist only in your subconscious mind, where their presence will be hard to detect.

Remember, too, as you analyze the "Six Ghosts of Fear," that they are nothing but ghosts because they exist only in one's mind.

Remember, also, that ghosts—creations of uncontrolled imagination—have caused most of the damage people have done to their own minds, therefore, ghosts can be as dangerous as if they lived and walked on the earth in physical bodies.

Notes

All of the universe operates through law. Our mind is no exception, and Think and Grow Rich is a guide to using those laws for achieving our chief aim in life.

Just as electricity has a set of laws, that if not followed, will not produce a result or worse will produce a harmful one, the mind follows a set of laws as well. To just read Think and Grow Rich and not practice the techniques laid out for achieving success, will not result in success, or worse, it could make it harder for one to achieve success.

Look around, not just electricity, but other natural forces all follow an order or law for manifestation. Gravity, atomic energy, magnetism, solar energy, all follow a natural order. As our mind is a part of nature, it too follows a natural order, and when that order and the laws contained within it are followed, achieving one's desires becomes as easy as turning on a light switch.

The difficulties that most people experience in achieving their desires and chief purpose in life are because they have not clearly stated what their desires and chief aim in life are, created a plan to achieve them, and carried through with their plan using persistence.

If you have done the exercises contained within this workbook, at minimum you should know what your chief aim and desires are at this point in your life. It is up to you to make a plan and follow through with that plan. If your plan does not work, create a new one and apply that plan. It is through the persistence of executing your plans that ultimately leads to your chief aim being fulfilled.

Chapter 15 - How To Outwit The Six Ghosts Of Fear

Review

Take Inventory of Yourself, As You Read This Closing Chapter, and Find Out How Many of the "Ghosts" Are Standing in Your Way

BEFORE you can put any portion of this philosophy into successful use, your mind must be prepared to receive it. The preparation is not difficult. It begins with study, analysis, and understanding of three enemies which you shall have to clear out. These are INDECISION, DOUBT, and FEAR!

The Sixth Sense will never function while these three negatives, or any of them remain in your mind. The members of this unholy trio are closely related; where one is found, the other two are close at hand.

INDECISION is the seedling of FEAR! Remember this, as you read. Indecision crystallizes into DOUBT, the two blend and become FEAR! The "blending" process often is slow. This is one reason why these three enemies are so dangerous. They germinate and grow without their presence being observed.

The remainder of this chapter describes an end which must be attained before the philosophy, as a whole, can be put into practical use. It also analyzes a condition which has, but lately, reduced huge numbers of people to poverty, and it states a truth which must be understood by all who accumulate riches, whether measured in terms of money or a state of mind of far greater value than money. The purpose of this chapter is to turn the spotlight of attention upon the cause and the cure of the six basic fears. Before we can master an enemy, we must know its name, its habits, and its place of abode. As you read, analyze yourself carefully, and determine which, if any, of the six common fears have attached themselves to you.

Do not be deceived by the habits of these subtle enemies. Sometimes they remain hidden in the subconscious mind, where they are difficult to locate, and still more difficult to eliminate.

There are six basic fears, with some combination of which every human suffers at one time or another. Most people are fortunate if they do not suffer from the entire six. Named in the order of their most common appearance, they are:

Named in the order of their most common appearance, they are:—

> The fear of POVERTY   } at the bottom of
> The fear of CRITICISM   } most of one's
> The fear of ILL HEALTH   } worries
>
> The fear of LOSS OF LOVE OF SOMEONE
> The fear of OLD AGE
> The fear of DEATH

All other fears are of minor importance, they can be grouped under these six headings.

Fears are nothing more than states of mind. One's state of mind is subject to control and direction. Physicians, as everyone knows, are less subject to attack by disease than ordinary laymen, for the reason that physicians DO NOT FEAR DISEASE. Physicians, without fear or hesitation, have been known to physically contact *hundreds of people, daily, who were suffering from such contagious diseases as small-pox, without becoming infected. Their immunity against the disease consisted, largely, if not solely, in their absolute lack of FEAR.*

Man can create nothing which he does not first conceive in the form of an impulse of thought.

MAN'S THOUGHT IMPULSES BEGIN IMMEDIATELY TO TRANSLATE THEMSELVES INTO THEIR PHYSICAL EQUIVALENT, WHETHER THOSE THOUGHTS ARE VOLUNTARY OR INVOLUNTARY.

We are here laying the foundation for the presentation of a fact of great importance to the person who does not understand why some people appear to be "lucky" while others of equal or greater ability, training, experience, and brain capacity, seem destined to ride with misfortune. This fact may be explained by the statement that every human being has the ability to completely control his own mind, and with this control, obviously, every person may open his mind to the tramp thought impulses which are being released by other brains, or close the doors tightly and admit only thought impulses of his own choice.

Nature has endowed man with absolute control over but one thing, and that is THOUGHT. This fact, coupled with the additional fact that everything which man creates, begins in the form of a thought, leads one very near to the principle by which FEAR may be mastered.

If it is true that ALL THOUGHT HAS A TENDENCY TO CLOTHE ITSELF IN ITS PHYSICAL EQUIVALENT (and this is true, beyond any reasonable room for doubt), it is equally true that thought impulses of fear and poverty cannot be translated into terms of courage and financial gain.

If you want riches, you must refuse to accept any circumstance that leads toward poverty.

If you demand riches, determine what form, and how much will be required to satisfy you. You know the road that leads to riches. You have been given a road map which, if followed, will keep you on that road. If you neglect to make the start, or stop before you arrive, no one will be to blame, but YOU. This responsibility is yours. No alibi will save you from accepting the responsibility if you now fail or refuse to demand riches of Life, because the acceptance calls for but one thing—incidentally, the only thing you can control—and that is a STATE OF MIND. A state of mind is something that one assumes. It cannot be purchased, it must be created.

This fear paralyzes the faculty of reason, destroys the faculty of imagination, kills off self-reliance, undermines enthusiasm, discourages initiative, leads to uncertainty of purpose, encourages procrastination, wipes out enthusiasm and makes self-control an impossibility. It takes the charm from one's personality, destroys the possibility of accurate thinking, diverts concentration of effort, it masters persistence, turns the will-power into nothingness, destroys ambition, beclouds the memory and invites failure in every conceivable form; it kills love and assassinates the finer emotions of the heart, discourages friendship and invites disaster in a hundred forms, leads to sleeplessness, misery and unhappiness—and all this despite the obvious truth that we live in a world of over-abundance of everything the heart could desire, with nothing standing between us and our desires, excepting lack of a definite purpose.

The Fear of Poverty is, without doubt, the most destructive of the six basic fears. It has been placed at the head of the list, because it is the most difficult to master. Considerable courage is required to state the truth about the origin of this fear, and still greater courage to accept the truth after it has been stated. The fear of poverty grew out of man's inherited tendency to PREY UPON HIS FELLOW MAN ECONOMICALLY. Nearly all animals lower than man are motivated by instinct, but their capacity to "think" is limited, therefore, they prey upon one another physically. Man, with his superior sense of intuition, with the capacity to think and to reason,

does not eat his fellow man bodily, he gets more satisfaction out of "eating" him FINANCIALLY. Man is so avaricious that every
conceivable law has been passed to safeguard him from his fellow man.

Of all the ages of the world, of which we know anything, the age in which we live seems to be one that is outstanding because of man's money-madness. A man is considered less than the dust of the earth, unless he can display a fat bank account; but if he has money—NEVER MIND HOW HE ACQUIRED IT—he is a "king" or a "big shot"; he is above the law, he rules in politics, he dominates in business, and the whole world about him bows in respect when he passes.

Nothing brings man so much suffering and humility as POVERTY! Only those who have experienced poverty understand the full meaning of this.

It is no wonder that man fears poverty. Through a long line of inherited experiences man has learned, for sure, that some men cannot be trusted, where matters of money and earthly possessions are concerned. This is a rather stinging indictment, the worst part of it being that it is TRUE.

So eager is man to possess wealth that he will acquire it in whatever manner he can—through legal methods if possible-through other methods if necessary or expedient.

Self-analysis may disclose weaknesses which one does not like to acknowledge. This form of examination is essential to all who demand of Life more than mediocrity and poverty. Remember, as you check yourself point by point, that you are both the court and the jury, the prosecuting attorney and the attorney for the defense, and that you are the plaintiff and the defendant, also, that you are on trial. Face the facts squarely. Ask yourself definite questions and demand direct replies. When the examination is over, you will know more about yourself. If you do not feel that you can be an impartial judge in this self-examination, call upon someone who knows you well to serve as judge while you cross-examine yourself. You are after the truth. Get it, no matter at what cost even though it may temporarily embarrass you!

The majority of people, if asked what they fear most, would reply, "I fear nothing." The reply would be inaccurate, because few people realize that they are bound, handicapped, whipped spiritually and physically through some form of fear. So subtle and deeply seated is the emotion of fear that one may go through life burdened with it, never recognizing its presence. Only a courageous analysis will disclose the presence of this universal enemy. When you begin such an analysis, search deeply into your character.

SYMPTOMS OF THE FEAR OF POVERTY

INDIFFERENCE. Commonly expressed through lack of ambition; willingness to tolerate poverty; acceptance of whatever compensation life may offer without protest; mental and physical laziness; lack of initiative, imagination, enthusiasm and self-control .

INDECISION. The habit of permitting others to do one's thinking. Staying "on the fence."

DOUBT. Generally expressed through alibis and excuses designed to cover up, explain away, or apologize for one's failures, sometimes expressed in the form of envy of those who are successful, or by criticising them.
WORRY. Usually expressed by finding fault with others, a tendency to spend beyond one's income, neglect of personal appearance, scowling and frowning; intemperance in the use of alcoholic drink, sometimes through the use of narcotics; nervousness, lack of poise, self-consciousness and lack of self-reliance.

OVER-CAUTION. The habit of looking for the negative side of every circumstance, thinking and talking of possible failure instead of concentrating upon the means of succeeding. Knowing all the roads to disaster, but never searching for the plans to avoid failure. Waiting for "the right time" to begin putting ideas and plans into action, until the waiting becomes a permanent habit. Remembering those who have failed, and forgetting those who have succeeded. Seeing the hole in the doughnut, but overlooking the doughnut. Pessimism, leading to indigestion, poor elimination, auto-intoxication, bad breath and bad disposition.

PROCRASTINATION. The habit of putting off until tomorrow that which should have been done last year. Spending enough time in creating alibis and excuses to have done the job. This symptom is closely related to over-caution, doubt and worry. Refusal to accept responsibility when it can be avoided. Willingness to compromise rather than put up a stiff fight. Compromising with difficulties instead of harnessing and using them as stepping stones to advancement. Bargaining with Life for a penny, instead of demanding prosperity, opulence, riches, contentment and happiness. Planning what to do IF AND WHEN OVERTAKEN BY FAILURE, INSTEAD OF BURNING ALL BRIDGES AND MAKING RETREAT IMPOSSIBLE. Weakness of, and often total lack of self-confidence, definiteness of purpose, self-control, initiative, enthusiasm, ambition, thrift and sound reasoning ability. EXPECTING POVERTY INSTEAD OF DEMANDING RICHES. Association with those who accept poverty instead of seeking the company of those who demand and receive riches.

When a man is down and out and on the street, unable to get any job at all, something happens to his spirit which can be observed in the droop of his shoulders, the set of his hat, his walk and his gaze. He cannot escape a feeling of inferiority among people with regular employment, even though he knows they are definitely not his equals in character, intelligence or ability.
"These people—even his friends—feel, on the other hand, a sense of superiority and regard him, perhaps unconsciously, as a casualty. He may borrow for a time, but not enough to carry on in his accustomed way, and he cannot continue to borrow very long. But borrowing in itself, when a man is borrowing merely to live, is a depressing experience, and the money lacks the power of earned money to revive his spirits. Of course, none of this applies to bums or habitual ne'er-do-wells, but only to men of normal ambitions and self-respect.

THE FEAR OF CRITICISM

This author, being neither a humorist nor a prophet, is inclined to attribute the basic fear of criticism to that part of man's inherited nature which prompts him not only to take away his fellow man's goods and wares, but to justify his action by CRITICISM of his fellow man's character.

The fear of criticism takes on many forms, the majority of which are petty and trivial.

The astute manufacturers of clothing have not been slow to capitalize this basic fear of criticism, with which all mankind has been cursed. Every season the styles in many articles of wearing apparel change. Who establishes the styles? Certainly not the purchaser of clothing, but the manufacturer. Why does he change the styles so often? The answer is obvious. He changes the styles so he can sell more clothes. For the same reason the manufacturers of automobiles (with a few rare and very sensible exceptions) change styles of models every
season. No man wants to drive an automobile which is not of the latest style, although the older model may actually be the better car.

We have been describing the manner in which people behave under the influence of fear of criticism as applied to the small and petty things of life. Let us now examine human behavior when this fear affects people in connection with the more important events of human relationship. Take for example practically any person who *has reached the age of "mental maturity" (from 35 to 40 years of age, as a general average), and if you could read the secret thoughts of his mind, you would find a very decided disbelief in most of the fables taught by the majority of the dogmatists and theologians a few decades back.*

Not often, however, will you find a person who has the courage to openly state his belief on this subject. Most people will, if pressed far enough, tell a lie rather than admit that they do not believe the stories associated with that form of religion which held people in bondage prior to the age of scientific discovery and education.

Why does the average person, even in this day of enlightenment, shy away from denying his belief in the fables which were the basis of most of the religions a few decades ago? The answer is, "because of the fear of criticism." Men and women have been burned at the stake for daring to express disbelief in ghosts. It is no wonder we have inherited a consciousness which makes us fear criticism. The time was, and not so far in the past, when criticism carried severe punishments-it still does in some countries.

The fear of criticism robs man of his initiative, destroys his power of imagination, limits his individuality, takes away his self-reliance, and does him damage in a hundred other ways. Parents often do their children irreparable injury by criticising them.

Criticism is the one form of service, of which everyone has too much. Everyone has a stock of it which is handed out, gratis, whether called for or not. One's nearest relatives often are the worst offenders. It should be recognized as a crime (in reality it is a crime of the worst nature), for any parent to build inferiority complexes in the mind of a child, through unnecessary criticism. Employers who understand human nature, get the best there is in men, not by criticism, but by constructive suggestion. Parents may accomplish the same results with their children. Criticism will plant FEAR in the human heart, or resentment, but it will not build love or affection.

SYMPTOMS OF THE FEAR OF CRITICISM

This fear is almost as universal as the fear of poverty, and its effects are just as fatal to personal achievement, mainly because this fear destroys initiative, and discourages the use of imagination.

SELF-CONSCIOUSNESS. Generally expressed through nervousness, timidity in conversation and in meeting strangers, awkward movement of the hands and limbs, shifting of the eyes.

LACK OF POISE. Expressed through lack of voice control, nervousness in the presence of others, poor posture of body, poor memory.

PERSONALITY. Lacking in firmness of decision, personal charm, and ability to express opinions definitely. The habit of side-stepping issues instead of meeting them squarely. Agreeing with others without careful examination of their opinions.

INFERIORITY COMPLEX. The habit of expressing self-approval by word of mouth and by actions, as a means of covering up a feeling of inferiority. Using "big words" to impress others, (often without knowing the real meaning of the words). Imitating others in dress, speech and manners. Boasting of imaginary achievements. This sometimes gives a surface appearance of a feeling of superiority.
EXTRAVAGANCE. The habit of trying to "keep up with the Joneses," spending beyond one's income.

LACK OF INITIATIVE. Failure to embrace opportunities for self-advancement, fear to express opinions, lack of confidence in one's own ideas, giving evasive answers to questions asked by superiors, hesitancy of manner and speech, deceit in both words and deeds.

LACK OF AMBITION. Mental and physical laziness, lack of self-assertion, slowness in reaching decisions, easily influenced by others, the habit of criticising others behind their backs and flattering them to their faces, the habit of accepting defeat without protest, quitting an undertaking when opposed by others, suspicious of other people without cause, lacking in tactfulness of manner and speech, unwillingness to accept the blame for mistakes.

THE FEAR OF ILL HEALTH

It is closely associated, as to its origin, with the causes of fear of Old Age and the fear of Death, because it leads one closely to the border of "terrible worlds" of which man knows not, but concerning which he has been taught some discomforting stories.

In the main, man fears ill health because of the terrible pictures which have been planted in his mind of what may happen if death should overtake him. He also fears it because of the economic toll which it may claim.

It has been shown most convincingly that the fear of disease, even where there is not the slightest cause for fear, often produces the physical symptoms of the disease feared.

Powerful and mighty is the human mind! It builds or it destroys.

There is overwhelming evidence that disease sometimes begins in the form of negative thought impulse.

The seed of fear of ill health lives in every human mind. Worry, fear, discouragement, disappointment in love and business affairs all cause this seed to germinate and grow.

Disappointments in business and in love stand at the head of the list of causes of fear of ill health.

SYMPTOMS OF THE FEAR OF ILL HEALTH

AUTO-SUGGESTION. The habit of negative use of self-suggestion by looking for, and expecting to find the symptoms of all kinds of disease. "Enjoying" imaginary illness and speaking of it as being real. The habit of trying all "fads" and "isms" recommended by others as having therapeutic value. Talking to others of operations, accidents and other forms of illness. Experimenting with diets, physical exercises, reducing systems, without professional guidance. Trying home remedies, patent medicines and "quack" remedies.

HYPOCHONDRIA. The habit of talking of illness, concentrating the mind upon disease, and expecting its appearance until a nervous break occurs. Nothing that comes in bottles can cure this condition. It is brought on by negative thinking and nothing but positive thought can affect a cure. Hypochondria, (a medical term for imaginary disease) is said to do as much damage on occasion, as the disease one fears might do. Most so-called cases of "nerves" come from imaginary illness.

EXERCISE. Fear of ill health often interferes with proper physical exercise, and results in over-weight, by causing one to avoid outdoor life.
SUSCEPTIBILITY. Fear of ill health breaks down Nature's body resistance, and creates a favorable condition for any form of disease one may contact.

SELF-CODDLING. The habit of making a bid for sympathy, using imaginary illness as the lure. (People often resort to this trick to avoid work). The habit of feigning illness to cover plain laziness, or to serve as an alibi for lack of ambition.

INTEMPERANCE. The habit of using alcohol or narcotics to destroy pains such as headaches, neuralgia, etc., instead of eliminating the cause.

The habit of reading about illness and worrying over the possibility of being stricken by it. The habit of reading patent medicine advertisements.

THE FEAR OF LOSS OF LOVE

Jealousy, and other similar forms of dementia praecox grow out of man's inherited fear of the loss of love of someone. This fear is the most painful of all the six basic fears. It probably plays more havoc with the body and mind than any of the other basic fears, as it often leads to permanent insanity.

Careful analysis has shown that women are more susceptible to this fear than men. This fact is easily explained. Women have learned, from experience, that men are polygamous by nature, that they are not to be trusted in the hands of rivals.

SYMPTOMS OF THE FEAR OF LOSS OF LOVE

JEALOUSY. The habit of being suspicious of friends and loved ones without any reasonable evidence of sufficient grounds. (Jealousy is a form of dementia praecox which sometimes becomes violent without the slightest cause). The habit of accusing wife or husband of infidelity without grounds. General suspicion of everyone, absolute faith in no one.

FAULT FINDING. The habit of finding fault with friends, relatives, business associates and loved ones upon the slightest provocation, or without any cause whatsoever.

GAMBLING. The habit of gambling, stealing, cheating, and otherwise taking hazardous chances to provide money for loved ones, with the belief that love can be bought. The habit of spending beyond one's means, or incurring debts, to provide gifts for loved ones, with the object of making a favorable showing. Insomnia, nervousness, lack of persistence, weakness of will, lack of self-control, lack of self-reliance, bad temper.

THE FEAR OF OLD AGE

In the main, this fear grows out of two sources. First, the thought that old age may bring with it POVERTY. Secondly, and by far the most common source of origin, from false and cruel teachings of the past which have been too well mixed with "fire and brimstone," and other bogies cunningly designed to enslave man through fear.

The possibility of ill health, which is more common as people grow older, is also a contributing cause of this common fear of old age. Eroticism also enters into the cause of the fear of old age, as no man cherishes the thought of diminishing sex attraction.

The most common cause of fear of old age is associated with the possibility of poverty.

Another contributing cause of the fear of old age, is the possibility of loss of freedom and independence, as old age may bring with it the loss of both physical and economic freedom.

SYMPTOMS OF THE FEAR OF OLD AGE

The tendency to slow down and develop an inferiority complex at the age of mental maturity, around the age of forty, falsely believing one's self to be "slipping" because of age. (The truth is that man's most useful years, mentally and spiritually, are those between forty and sixty).

The habit of speaking apologetically of one's self as "being old" merely because one has reached the age of forty, or fifty, instead of reversing the rule and expressing gratitude for having reached the age of wisdom and understanding.

The habit of killing off initiative, imagination, and self-reliance by falsely believing one's self too old to exercise these qualities. The habit of the man or woman of forty dressing with the aim of trying to appear much younger, and affecting mannerisms of youth; thereby inspiring ridicule by both friends and strangers.

THE FEAR OF DEATH

To some this is the cruelest of all the basic fears. The reason is obvious. The terrible pangs of fear associated with the thought of death, in the majority of cases, may be charged directly to religious fanaticism. So-called "heathen" are less afraid of death than the more "civilized." For hundreds of millions of years man has been asking the still unanswered questions, "whence" and "whither." Where did I come from, and where am I going?

During the darker ages of the past, the more cunning and crafty were not slow to offer the answer to these questions, FOR A PRICE. Witness, now, the major source of origin of the FEAR OF DEATH.

"Come into my tent, embrace my faith, accept my dogmas, and I will give you a ticket that will admit you straightaway into heaven when you die," cries a leader of sectarianism. "Remain out of my tent," says the same leader, "and may the devil take you and burn you throughout eternity."

ETERNITY is a long time. FIRE is a terrible thing. The thought of eternal punishment, with fire, not only causes man to fear death, it often causes him to lose his reason. It destroys interest in life and makes happiness impossible.

In truth, NO MAN KNOWS, and no man has ever known, what heaven or hell is like, nor does any man know if either place actually exists. This very lack of positive knowledge opens the door of the human mind to the charlatan so he may enter and control that mind with his stock of legerdemain and various brands of pious fraud and trickery.

The fear of DEATH is not as common now as it was during the age when there were no great colleges and universities. Men of science have turned the spotlight of truth upon the world, and this truth is rapidly freeing men and women from this terrible fear of DEATH. The young men and young women who attend the colleges and universities are not easily impressed by "fire" and "brimstone." Through the aid of biology, astronomy, geology, and other related sciences, the fears of the dark ages which gripped the minds of men and destroyed their reason have been dispelled.
This fear is useless. Death will come, no matter what anyone may think about it. Accept it as a necessity, and pass the thought out of your mind. It must be a, necessity, or it would not come to all.

The entire world is made up of only two things, ENERGY and MATTER. In elementary physics we learn that neither matter nor energy (the only two realities known to man) can be created nor destroyed. Both matter and energy can be transformed, but neither can be destroyed.

Life is energy, if it is anything. If neither energy nor matter can be destroyed, of course life cannot be destroyed. Life, like other forms of energy, may be passed through various processes of transition, or change, but it cannot be destroyed. Death is mere transition.

If death is not mere change, or transition, then nothing comes after death except a long, eternal, peaceful sleep, and sleep is nothing to be feared. Thus you may wipe out, forever, the fear of Death.

SYMPTOMS OF THE FEAR OF DEATH

The general symptoms of this fear are:

The habit of THINKING about dying instead of making the most of LIFE, due, generally, to lack of purpose, or lack of a suitable occupation. This fear is more prevalent among the aged, but sometimes the more youthful are victims of it. The greatest of all remedies for the fear of death is a BURNING DESIRE FOR ACHIEVEMENT, backed by useful service to others. A busy person seldom has time to think about dying. He finds life too thrilling to worry about death. Sometimes the fear of death is closely associated with the Fear of Poverty, where one's death would leave loved ones poverty-stricken. In other cases, the fear of death is caused by illness and the consequent breaking down of physical body resistance. The commonest causes of the fear of death are: ill-health, poverty, lack of appropriate occupation, disappointment over love, insanity, religious fanaticism.

OLD MAN WORRY

Worry is a state of mind based upon fear. It works slowly, but persistently. It is insidious and subtle. Step by step it "digs itself in" until it paralyzes one's reasoning faculty, destroys self-confidence and initiative. Worry is a form of sustained fear caused by indecision therefore it is a state of mind which can be controlled.

An unsettled mind is helpless. Indecision makes an unsettled mind.

We do not worry over conditions, once we have reached a decision to follow a definite line of action.

The six basic fears become translated into a state of worry, through indecision. Relieve yourself, forever of the fear of death, by reaching a decision to accept death as an inescapable event. Whip the fear of poverty by reaching a decision to get along with whatever wealth you can accumulate WITHOUT WORRY. Put your foot upon the neck of the fear of criticism by reaching a decision NOT TO WORRY about what other people think, do, or say. Eliminate the fear of old age by reaching a decision to accept it, not as a handicap, but as a great blessing which carries with it wisdom, self-control, and understanding not known to youth.

Acquit yourself of the fear of ill health by the decision to forget symptoms. Master the fear of loss of love by reaching a decision to get along without love, if that is necessary.
Kill the habit of worry, in all its forms, by reaching a general, blanket decision that nothing which life has to offer is worth the price of worry. With this decision will come poise, peace of mind, and calmness of thought which will bring happiness.

A man whose mind is filled with fear not only destroys his own chances of intelligent action, but, he transmits these destructive vibrations to the minds of all who come into contact with him, and destroys, also their chances.

The person who gives expression, by word of mouth, to negative or destructive thoughts is practically certain to experience the results of those words in the form of a destructive "kick-back." The release of destructive thought impulses, alone, without the aid of words, produces also a "kickback" in more ways than one. First of all, and perhaps most important to be remembered, the person who releases thoughts of a destructive nature, must suffer damage through the breaking down of the faculty of creative imagination. Secondly, the presence in the mind of any destructive emotion develops a negative personality which repels people, and often converts them into antagonists. The third source of damage to the person who entertains or releases negative thoughts, lies in this significant fact—these thought-impulses are not only damaging to others, but they IMBED THEMSELVES IN THE SUBCONSCIOUS MIND OF THE PERSON RELEASING THEM, and there become a part of his character.

One is never through with a thought, merely by releasing it. When a thought is released, it spreads in every direction, through the medium of the ether, but it also plants itself permanently in the subconscious mind of the person releasing it.

Your business in life is, presumably to achieve success. To be successful, you must find peace of mind, acquire the material needs of life, and above all, attain HAPPINESS. All of these evidences of success begin in the form of thought impulses.

You may control your own mind, you have the power to feed it whatever thought impulses you choose. With this privilege goes also the responsibility of using it constructively. You are the master of your own earthly destiny just as surely as you have the power to control your own thoughts. You may influence, direct, and eventually control your own environment, making your life what you want it to be—or, you may neglect to exercise the privilege which is yours, to make your life to order, thus casting yourself upon the broad sea of "Circumstance" where you will be tossed hither and yon, like a chip on the waves of the ocean.

The Seventh Basic Evil

In addition to the Six Basic Fears, there is another evil by which people suffer. It constitutes a rich soil in which the seeds of failure grow abundantly. It is so subtle that its presence often is not detected. This affliction cannot properly be classed as a fear. IT IS MORE DEEPLY SEATED AND MORE OFTEN FATAL THAN ALL OF THE SIX FEARS. For want of a better name, let us call this evil SUSCEPTIBILITY TO NEGATIVE INFLUENCES.

If you are reading this philosophy for the purpose of accumulating riches, you should examine yourself very carefully, to determine whether you are susceptible to negative influences. If you neglect this self-analysis, you will forfeit your right to attain the object of your desires.

Make the analysis searching. After you read the questions prepared for this self-analysis, hold yourself to a strict accounting in your answers. Go at the task as carefully as you would search for any other enemy you knew to be awaiting you in ambush and deal with your own faults as you would with a more tangible enemy.

The "seventh basic evil" is more difficult to master, because it strikes when you are not aware of its presence, when you are asleep, and while you are awake. Moreover, its weapon is intangible, because it consists of merely—a STATE OF MIND. This evil is also dangerous because it strikes in as many different forms as there are human experiences. Sometimes it enters the mind through the well-meant words of one's own relatives. At other times, it bores from within, through one's own mental attitude. Always it is as deadly as poison, even though it may not kill as quickly.

HOW TO PROTECT YOURSELF AGAINST NEGATIVE INFLUENCES

To protect yourself against negative influences, whether of your own making, or the result of the activities of negative people around you, recognize that you have a WILL-POWER, and put it into constant use, until it builds a wall of immunity against negative influences in your own mind.

Recognize the fact that you, and every other human being, are, by nature, lazy, indifferent, and susceptible to all suggestions which harmonize with your weaknesses.

Recognize that you are, by nature, susceptible to all the six basic fears, and set up. habits for the purpose of counteracting all these fears.

Recognize that negative influences often work on you through your subconscious mind, therefore they are difficult to detect, and keep your mind closed against all people who depress or discourage you in any way.

Deliberately seek the company of people who influence you to THINK AND ACT FOR YOURSELF.

Do not EXPECT troubles as they have a tendency not to disappoint.

Without doubt, the most common weakness of all human beings is the habit of leaving their minds open to the negative influence of other people. This weakness is all the more damaging, because most people do not recognize that they are cursed by it, and many who acknowledge it, neglect or refuse to correct the evil until it becomes an uncontrollable part of their daily habits.

If you have answered all these questions truthfully, you know more about yourself than the majority of people. Study the questions carefully, come back to them once each week for several months, and be astounded at the amount of additional knowledge of great value to yourself, you will have gained by the simple method of answering the questions truthfully. If you are not certain concerning the answers to some of the questions, seek the counsel of those who know you well, especially those who have no motive in flattering you, and see yourself through their eyes. The experience will be astonishing.

You have ABSOLUTE CONTROL over but one thing, and that is your thoughts. This is the most significant and inspiring of all facts known to man! It reflects man's Divine nature. This Divine prerogative is the sole means by which you may control your own destiny.

If you fail to control your own mind, you may be sure you will control nothing else.
If you must be careless with your possessions, let it be in connection with material things. Your mind is your spiritual estate! Protect and use it with the care to which Divine Royalty is entitled. You were given a WILLPOWER for this purpose.

Men with negative minds tried to convince Thomas A. Edison that he could not build a machine that would record and reproduce the human voice, "because" they said, "no one else had ever produced such a machine." Edison did not believe them. He knew that the mind could produce ANYTHING THE MIND COULD CONCEIVE AND BELIEVE, and that knowledge was the thing that lifted the great Edison above the common herd.

For the benefit of those seeking vast riches, let it be remembered that practically the sole difference between Henry Ford and a majority of the more than one hundred thousand men who work for him, is this-FORD HAS A MIND AND CONTROLS IT, THE OTHERS HAVE MINDS WHICH THEY DO NOT TRY TO CONTROL.

His record knocks the foundation from under that time-worn alibi, "I never had a chance." Ford never had a chance, either, but he CREATED AN OPPORTUNITY AND BACKED IT WITH PERSISTENCE UNTIL IT MADE HIM RICHER THAN CROESUS.

Mind control is the result of self-discipline and habit. You either control your mind or it controls you. There is no hall-way compromise. The most practical of all methods for controlling the mind is the habit of keeping it busy with a definite purpose, backed by a definite plan.

Study the record of any man who achieves noteworthy success, and you will observe that he has control over his own mind, moreover, that he exercises that control and directs it toward the attainment of definite objectives. Without this control, success is not possible.

Building alibis is a deeply rooted habit. Habits are difficult to break, especially when they provide justification for something we do. Plato had this truth in mind when he said, "The first and best victory is to conquer self. To be conquered by self is, of all things, the most shameful and vile."

Another philosopher had the same thought in mind when he said, "It was a great surprise to me when I discovered that most of the ugliness I saw in others, was but a reflection of my own nature."

"It has always been a mystery to me," said Elbert Hubbard, "why people spend so much time deliberately fooling themselves by creating alibis to cover their weaknesses. If used differently, this same time would be sufficient to cure the weakness, then no alibi would be needed.

"Life is a checkerboard, and the player opposite you is TIME. If you hesitate before moving, or neglect to move promptly, your men will be wiped off the board by TIME. You are playing against a partner who will not tolerate INDECISION!"

Previously you may have had a logical excuse for not having forced Life to come through with whatever you asked, but that alibi is now obsolete, because you are in possession of the Master Key that unlocks the door to Life's bountiful riches.

The Master Key is intangible, but it is powerful! It is the privilege of creating, in your own mind, a BURNING DESIRE for a definite form of riches. There is no penalty for the use of the Key, but there is a price you must pay if you do not use it. The price is FAILURE. There is a reward of stupendous proportions if you put the Key to use. It is the satisfaction that comes to all who conquer self and force Life to pay whatever is asked.

The reward is worthy of your effort. Will you make the start and be convinced?

Notes

You have reached the end of the text, but not the end of the work. The philosophy of Think and Grow Rich is something that must be worked on all the time, and though breaks are deserved and required, it is important that you use this material continuously so you can achieve your current desires, and future ones you have not even thought about yet.

The following appendix includes several self inventory analyses from the book. I have collected them in one location so you could go through each one and build off the previous one. It also makes it easy to find for subsequent inventories. It is important that you complete them now, and schedule a regular interval, (no longer than a year) to go through them again. I suggest you choose a day where you have most of the day to go over and considered the inventories. They take a commitment to be honest with yourself and could bring up corresponding emotions/feelings.

Exercise

Read over the inventory questions and statements in the appendix and schedule a day within the next two weeks that you can complete the inventories. Schedule the whole day, as it will take most of it to take and honestly complete the inventory.

Do not put this off, as this is one of the most crucial exercises within the Think and Grow Rich course. It is when we can be honest with ourselves, take an honest look at who we are, and commit to who we want to become that real change will start to manifest itself in your life.

Write down the date in your calendar now, and choose the date you are going to follow up. Don't do follow up inventories more frequent than once a month nor any longer than once a year.

I suggest you use a notebook and save your results, as you will use them as a reference point to track for yourself the changes that have come about because of your commitment to yourself and desires.

Appendix

The Thirty Major Causes Of Failure
How Many Of These Are Holding You Back?

Napoleon Hill interviewed thousands of people while preparing the material for Think and Grow Rich and in doing so, he was able to compile a list of the thirty major causes of failure. Though he makes it clear that each one can be overcome, he provided the list so one could take inventory of themselves and discover how many of these items stood between them and their success. Read over the list and check yourself by it, and take inventory of yourself so you can overcome anything standing between you and success. It will be helpful if you can have someone who knows you well to go over this list with you, and help to analyze you by the thirty causes of failure.

You should know all of your weaknesses in order that you may either bridge them or eliminate them entirely. You should know your strength in order that you may call attention to it when selling your services. You can know yourself only through accurate analysis.

1. _____**UNFAVORABLE HEREDITARY BACKGROUND.** There is but little, if anything, which can be done for people who are born with a deficiency in brain power. This philosophy offers but one method of bridging this weakness—through the aid of the Master Mind. Observe with profit, however, that this is the ONLY one of
the thirty causes of failure which may not be easily corrected by any individual.

2. _____**LACK OF A WELL-DEFINED PURPOSE IN LIFE.** There is no hope of success for the person who does not have a central purpose, or definite goal at which to aim. Ninety-eight out of every hundred of those whom I have analyzed, had no such aim.

3._____**LACK OF AMBITION TO AIM ABOVE MEDIOCRITY.** We offer no hope for the person who is so indifferent as not to want to get ahead in life, and who is not willing to pay the price.

4. _____**INSUFFICIENT EDUCATION.** This is a handicap which may be overcome with comparative ease. Experience has proven that the best-educated people are often those who are known as "self-made," or self-educated. It takes more than a college degree to make one a person of education. Any person who is educated is one who has learned to get whatever he wants in life without violating the rights of others. Education consists, not so much of knowledge, but of knowledge effectively and persistently APPLIED. Men are paid, not merely for what they know, but more particularly for WHAT THEY DO WITH THAT WHICH THEY KNOW.

5. _____**LACK OF SELF-DISCIPLINE.** Discipline comes through self-control. This means that one must control all negative qualities. Before you can control conditions, you must first control yourself. Self-mastery is the hardest job you will ever tackle. If you do not conquer self, you will be conquered by self. You may see at one and the same time both your best friend and your greatest enemy, by stepping in front of a mirror.

6. _____**ILL HEALTH.** No person may enjoy outstanding success without good health. Many of the causes of ill health are subject to mastery and control. These, in the main are:
        a. Overeating of foods not conducive to health
        b. Wrong habits of thought; giving expression to negatives.
        c. Wrong use of, and overindulgence in sex.

        d. Lack of proper physical exercise
        e. An inadequate supply of fresh air, due to improper breathing.

7. _____UNFAVORABLE ENVIRONMENTAL INFLUENCES DURING CHILDHOOD. "As the twig is bent, so shall the tree grow." Most people who have criminal tendencies acquire them as the result of bad environment, and improper associates during childhood.

8. _____PROCRASTINATION. This is one of the most common causes of failure. "Old Man Procrastination" stands within the shadow of every human being, waiting his opportunity to spoil one's chances of success. Most of us go through life as failures, because we are waiting for the "time to be right" to start doing something worthwhile. Do not wait. The time will never be "just right." Start where you stand, and work with whatever tools you may have at your command, and better tools will be found as you go along.

9. _____LACK OF PERSISTENCE. Most of us are good "starters" but poor "finishers" of everything we begin. Moreover, people are prone to give up at the first signs of defeat. There is no substitute for PERSISTENCE. The person who makes PERSISTENCE his watch-word, discovers that "Old Man Failure" finally becomes tired, and makes his departure. Failure cannot cope with PERSISTENCE.

10. _____NEGATIVE PERSONALITY. There is no hope of success for the person who repels people through a negative personality. Success comes through the application of POWER, and power is attained through the cooperative efforts of other people. A negative personality will not induce cooperation.

11. _____LACK OF CONTROLLED SEXUAL URGE. Sex energy is the most powerful of all the stimuli which move people into ACTION. Because it is the most powerful of the emotions, it must be controlled, through transmutation, and converted into other channels.

12. _____UNCONTROLLED DESIRE FOR "SOMETHING FOR NOTHING". The gambling instinct drives millions of people to failure. Evidence of this may be found in a study of the Wall Street crash of '29, during which millions of people tried to make money by gambling on stock margins.

13. _____LACK OF A WELL DEFINED POWER OF DECISION. Men who succeed reach decisions promptly, and change them, if at all, very slowly. Men who fail, reach decisions, if at all, very slowly, and change them frequently, and quickly. Indecision and procrastination are twin brothers. Where one is found, the other
may usually be found also. Kill off this pair before they completely "hog-tie" you to the treadmill of FAILURE.

14. _____ONE OR MORE OF THE SIX BASIC FEARS. These fears have been analyzed for you in a later chapter. They must be mastered before you can market your services effectively.

15. _____WRONG SELECTION OF A MATE IN MARRIAGE. This is the most common cause of failure. The relationship of marriage brings people intimately into contact. Unless this relationship is harmonious, failure is likely to follow. Moreover, it will be a form of failure that is marked by misery and unhappiness, destroying all signs of AMBITION.

16. _____OVER-CAUTION. The person who takes no chances, generally has to take whatever is left when others are through choosing. Over-caution is as bad as under-caution. Both are extremes to be guarded against. Life itself is filled with the element of chance.

17. _____WRONG SELECTION OF ASSOCIATES IN BUSINESS. This is one of the most common causes of failure in business. In marketing personal services, one should use great care to select an employer who will be an inspiration, and who is, himself, intelligent and successful. We emulate those with whom we associate most closely. Pick an employer who is worth emulating.

18. _____SUPERSTITION AND PREJUDICE. Superstition is a form of fear. It is also a sign of ignorance. Men who succeed keep open minds and are afraid of nothing.

19. _____WRONG SELECTION OF A VOCATION. No man can succeed in a line of endeavor which he does not like. The most essential step in the marketing of personal services is that of selecting an occupation into which you can throw yourself wholeheartedly.

20. _____LACK OF CONCENTRATION OF EFFORT. The "jack-of-all-trades" seldom is good at any. Concentrate all of your efforts on one DEFINITE CHIEF AIM.

21. _____THE HABIT OF INDISCRIMINATE SPENDING. The spendthrift cannot succeed, mainly because he stands eternally in FEAR OF POVERTY. Form the habit of systematic saving by putting aside a definite percentage of your income. Money in the bank gives one a very safe foundation of COURAGE when bargaining for the sale of personal services. Without money, one must take what one is offered, and be glad to get it.

22. _____LACK OF ENTHUSIASM. Without enthusiasm one cannot be convincing. Moreover, enthusiasm is contagious, and the person who has it, under control, is generally welcome in any group of people.

23. _____INTOLERANCE. The person with a "closed" mind on any subject seldom gets ahead. Intolerance means that one has stopped acquiring knowledge. The most damaging forms of intolerance are those connected with religious, racial, and political differences of opinion.

24. _____INTEMPERANCE. The most damaging forms of intemperance are connected with eating, strong drink, and sexual activities. Overindulgence in any of these is fatal to success.

25. _____INABILITY TO COOPERATE WITH OTHERS. More people lose their positions and their big opportunities in life, because of this fault, than for all other reasons combined. It is a fault which no well-informed business man, or leader will tolerate.

26. _____POSSESSION OF POWER THAT WAS NOT ACQUIRED THROUGH SELF EFFORT. (Sons and daughters of wealthy men, and others who inherit money which they did not earn). Power in the hands of one who did not acquire it gradually, is often fatal to success. QUICK RICHES are more dangerous than poverty.

27. _____INTENTIONAL DISHONESTY. There is no substitute for honesty. One may be temporarily dishonest by force of circumstances over which one has no control, without permanent damage. But, there is NO HOPE for the person who is dishonest by choice. Sooner or later, his deeds will catch up with him, and he will pay by loss of reputation, and perhaps even loss of liberty.

28. _____EGOTISM AND VANITY. These qualities serve as red lights which warn others to keep away. THEY ARE FATAL TO SUCCESS.

29. _____GUESSING INSTEAD OF THINKING. Most people are too indifferent or lazy to acquire FACTS with which to THINK ACCURATELY. They prefer to act on "opinions" created by guesswork or snap-judgments.

30. _____LACK OF CAPITAL. This is a common cause of failure among those who start out in business for the first time, without sufficient reserve of capital to absorb the shock of their mistakes, and to carry them over until they have established a REPUTATION.

Annual Self Analysis As Prescribed By Think and Grow Rich

Annual self-analysis is an essential in the effective marketing of personal services, as is annual inventory in merchandising. Moreover, the yearly analysis should disclose a DECREASE IN FAULTS, and an increase in VIRTUES. One goes ahead, stands still, or goes backward in life. One's object should be, of course, to go ahead. Annual self-analysis will disclose whether advancement has been made, and if so, how much. It will also disclose any backward steps one may have made. The effective marketing of personal services requires one to move forward even if the progress is slow. Your annual self-analysis should be made at the end of each year, so you can include in your New Year's Resolutions any improvements which the analysis indicates should be made. Take this inventory by asking yourself the following questions, and by checking your answers with the aid of someone who will not permit you to deceive yourself as to their accuracy.

SELF-ANALYSIS QUESTIONNAIRE FOR PERSONAL INVENTORY

Write your answers out on a separate sheet of paper and save it to compare to the following year's analysis.

Section1

1. Have I attained the goal which I established as my objective for this year? (You should work with a definite yearly objective to be attained as a part of your major life objective).

2. Have I delivered service of the best possible QUALITY of which I was capable, or could I have improved any part of this service?

3. Have I delivered service in the greatest possible QUANTITY of which I was capable?

4. Has the spirit of my conduct been harmonious, and cooperative at all times?

5. Have I permitted the habit of PROCRASTINATION to decrease my efficiency, and if so, to what extent?

6. Have I improved my PERSONALITY, and if so, in what ways?

7. Have I been PERSISTENT in following my plans through to completion?

8. Have I reached DECISIONS PROMPTLY AND DEFINITELY on all occasions?

9. Have I permitted any one or more of the six basic fears to decrease my efficiency?

10. Have I been either "over-cautious," or "under-cautious?"

11. Has my relationship with my associates in work been pleasant, or unpleasant? If it has been unpleasant, has the fault been partly, or wholly mine?

12. Have I dissipated any of my energy through lack of CONCENTRATION of effort?

13. Have I been open-minded and tolerant in connection with all subjects?

14. In what way have I improved my ability to render service?

15. Have I been intemperate in any of my habits?

16. Have I expressed, either openly or secretly, any form of EGOTISM?

17. Has my conduct toward my associates been such that it has induced them to RESPECT me?

18. Have my opinions and DECISIONS been based upon guesswork, or accuracy of analysis and THOUGHT?

19. Have I followed the habit of budgeting my time, my expenses, and my income, and have I been conservative in these budgets?

20. How much time have I devoted to UNPROFITABLE effort which I might have used to better advantage?

21. How may I RE-BUDGET my time, and change my habits so I will be more efficient during the coming year?

22. Have I been guilty of any conduct which was not approved by my conscience?

23. In what ways have I rendered MORE SERVICE AND BETTER SERVICE than I was paid to render?

24. Have I been unfair to anyone, and if so, in what way?

25. If I had been the purchaser of my own services for the year, would I be satisfied with my purchase?

26. Am I in the right vocation, and if not, why not?

27. Has the purchaser of my services been satisfied with the service I have rendered, and if not, why not?

28. What is my present rating on the fundamental principles of success? (Make this rating fairly, and frankly, and have it checked by someone who is courageous enough to do it accurately).

Section 2

1. Have you learned how to create a mental state of mind with which you can shield yourself against all discouraging influences?

2. Does your occupation inspire you with faith and hope?

3. Are you conscious of possessing spiritual forces of sufficient power to enable you to keep your mind free from all forms of FEAR?

4. Does your religion help you to keep your own mind positive?

5. Do you feel it your duty to share other people's worries? If so, why?

6. If you believe that "birds of a feather flock together" what have you learned about yourself by studying the friends whom you attract?

7. What connection, if any, do you see between the people with whom you associate most closely, and any unhappiness you may experience?

8. Could it be possible that some person whom you consider to be a friend is, in reality, your worst enemy, because of his negative influence on your mind?

9. By what rules do you judge who is helpful and who is damaging to you?

10. Are your intimate associates mentally superior or inferior to you?

11. How much time out of every 24 hours do you devote to:

    a. your occupation

    b. sleep

    c. play and relaxation

    d. acquiring useful knowledge

    e. plain waste

12. Who among your acquaintances:

    a. encourages you most

    b. cautions you most

    c. discourages you most

    d. helps you most in other ways

Section 3

1. Do you complain often of "feeling bad", and if so, what is the cause?

2. Do you find fault with other people at the slightest provocation?

3. Do you frequently make mistakes in your work, and if so, why?

4. Are you sarcastic and offensive in your conversation?

5. Do you deliberately avoid the association of anyone, and if so, why?

6. Do you suffer frequently with indigestion? If so, what is the cause?

7. Does life seem futile and the future hopeless to you? If so, why?

8. Do you like your occupation? If not, why?

9. Do you often feel self-pity, and if so why?

10. Are you envious of those who excel you?

11. To which do you devote most time, thinking of SUCCESS, or of FAILURE?

12. Are you gaining or losing self-confidence as you grow older?

13. Do you learn something of value from all mistakes?

14. Are you permitting some relative or acquaintance to worry you? If so, why?

15. Are you sometimes "in the clouds" and at other times in the depths of despondency?

16. Who has the most inspiring influence upon you? What is the cause?

17. Do you tolerate negative or discouraging influences which you can avoid?

18. Are you careless of your personal appearance? If so, when and why?

19. Have you learned how to "drown your troubles" by being too busy to be annoyed by them?

20. Would you call yourself a "spineless weakling" if you permitted others to do your thinking for you?

21. Do you neglect internal bathing until auto-intoxication makes you ill-tempered and irritable?

22. How many preventable disturbances annoy you, and why do you tolerate them?

23. Do you resort to liquor, narcotics, or cigarettes to "quiet your nerves"? If so, why do you not try will-power instead?

24. Does anyone "nag" you, and if so, for what reason?

25. Do you have a DEFINITE MAJOR PURPOSE, and if so, what is it, and what plan have you for achieving it?

26. Do you suffer from any of the Six Basic Fears? If so, which ones?

27. Have you a method by which you can shield yourself against the negative influence of others?

28. Do you make deliberate use of auto-suggestion to make your mind positive?

29. Which do you value most, your material possessions, or your privilege of controlling your own thoughts?

30. Are you easily influenced by others, against your own judgment?

31. Has today added anything of value to your stock of knowledge or state of mind?

32. Do you face squarely the circumstances which make you unhappy, or sidestep the responsibility?

33. Do you analyze all mistakes and failures and try to profit by them or, do you take the attitude that this is not your duty?

34. Can you name three of your most damaging weaknesses? What are you doing to correct them?

35. Do you encourage other people to bring their worries to you for sympathy?

36. Do you choose, from your daily experiences, lessons or influences which aid in your personal advancement?

37. Does your presence have a negative influence on other people as a rule?

38. What habits of other people annoy you most?

39. Do you form your own opinions or permit yourself to be influenced by other people?

40. What is your greatest worry? Why do you tolerate it?

41. When others offer you free, unsolicited advice, do you accept it without question, or analyze their motive?

42. What, above all else, do you most DESIRE? Do you intend to acquire it? Are you willing to subordinate all other desires for this one? How much time daily do you devote to acquiring it?

43. Do you change your mind often? If so, why?

44. Do you usually finish everything you begin?

45. Are you easily impressed by other people's business or professional titles, college degrees, or wealth?

46. Are you easily influenced by what other people think or say of you?

47. Do you cater to people because of their social or financial status?

48. Whom do you believe to be the greatest person living? In what respect is this person superior to yourself?

49. How much time have you devoted to studying and answering these questions?

(At least one day is necessary for the analysis and the answering of the entire list.)

"FIFTY-SEVEN" FAMOUS ALIBIS
By Old Man IF

People who do not succeed have one distinguishing trait in common. They know all the reasons for failure, and have what they believe to be air-tight alibis to explain away their own lack of achievement.

Some of these alibis are clever, and a few of them are justifiable by the facts. But alibis cannot be used for money. The world wants to know only one thing—HAVE YOU ACHIEVED SUCCESS?

Remember, too, the philosophy presented in this book makes every one of these alibis obsolete.

Place a check next to any alibi that you are guilty of using.

IF I didn't have a wife and family _____

IF I had enough "pull" _____

IF I had money _____

IF I had a good education _____

IF I could get a job _____

IF I had good health _____

IF I only had time _____

IF times were better _____

IF other people understood me _____

IF conditions around me were only different _____

IF I could live my life over again _____

IF I did not fear what "THEY" would say _____

IF I had been given a chance _____

IF I now had a chance _____

IF other people didn't "have it in for me" _____

IF nothing happens to stop me _____

IF I were only younger _____

IF I could only do what I want _____

IF I had been born rich _____

IF I could meet "the right people" _____

IF I had the talent that some people have _____

IF I dared assert myself _____

IF I only had embraced past opportunities _____

IF people didn't get on my nerves _____

IF I didn't have to keep house and look after the children _____

IF I could save some money _____

IF the boss only appreciated me _____

IF I only had somebody to help me _____

IF my family understood me _____

IF I lived in a big city _____

IF I could just get started _____

IF I were only free _____

IF I had the personality of some people _____

IF I were not so fat _____

IF my talents were known _____

IF I could just get a "break" _____

IF I could only get out of debt _____

IF I hadn't failed _____

IF I only knew how _____

IF everybody didn't oppose me _____

IF I didn't have so many worries _____

IF I could marry the right person _____

IF people weren't so dumb _____

IF my family were not so extravagant _____

IF I were sure of myself _____

IF luck were not against me _____

IF I had not been born under the wrong star _____

IF it were not true that "what is to be will be" _____

IF I did not have to work so hard _____

IF I hadn't lost my money _____

IF I lived in a different neighborhood _____

IF I didn't have a "past" _____

IF I only had a business of my own _____

IF other people would only listen to me _____

IF * * * and this is the greatest of them all * * * I had the courage to see myself as I really am, I would find out what is wrong with me, and correct it, then I might have a chance to profit by my mistakes and learn something from the experience of others, for I know that there is something WRONG with me, or I would now be where I WOULD HAVE BEEN IF I had spent more time analyzing my weaknesses, and less time building alibis to cover them.

Suggested Reading List

The following books are useful to read and study in addition to Think And Grow Rich. They are listed in particular order. There is room to write down any other books you find useful to study as well, so you can share the list with others.

The Science of The Mind by Ernest Holmes

The 4 Hour Workweek by Tim Ferris

The Evolution of Desire by David Buss

The Female Brain by Louann Brizendine

The Prophet by Kahlil Gibran

Edinburgh Lectures by Thomas Troward

As A Man Thinketh by James Allen

Power Vs Force by David Hawkins

The Eye of the I by David Hawkins

How to Win Friends and Influence People by Dale Carnegie

The Biology of Belief by Bruce Lipton

The following pages have been left blank on purpose, please fill them with your ideas, notes, lists, drawings and whatever other inspirations you may have. Best of luck to you!

Pinch

Punch

Puch

Pinch

Pitch

Pink

Pinch

Punch

Made in the USA
Lexington, KY
14 September 2018